Dare to Walk
IN THE SHOES DESIGNED FOR
YOU

by Nicole Jones

Sensual Steps Inc.
Chicago, IL
www.sensualstepsinc.com

Sensual Steps Inc.
4518 S. Cottage Grove
Chicago, IL 60653
First printing: December 14, 2010

Although the author and publisher have made every effort
to ensure the accuracy and completeness of information
contained in this book, we assume no responsibility for errors,
inaccuracies, omissions, or any inconsistencies therein.

Any slights, of people, places, belief systems or organizations
are unintentional. Any resemblance to anyone living,
dead or somewhere in between is coincidental.

ISBN: 978-0-615-42498-9

Edited by Marilyn Gilbert-Mitchell, Jorian Seay and Sarah Martin.
Interior Design by Scot Scott of Biohertz
Cover Photography by William Stokes
Cover Design by Scot Scott for www.Biohertz.com
Picture of men's shoes by Scott Dupart and Landis Cosmetics
Picture of ladies shoes by Luichiny

DEDICATION

This book is dedicated to the Johnson, McGee, Jones, Wheatly, Ingram and Hill families, as well as the youth that I've worked with at Gage Park, Orr Academy, Michelle Clark, and other Chicago Public Schools.

May our lives increase in prosperity always as we serve and bless others.

ACKNOWLEDGEMENTS

I give the highest and ultimate praise to the Lord, for He hath given me the breath to live day by day. It is only God's grace in my life that has helped me move mountains. I celebrate my mother and father who are the most dynamic parents in the world. I love them with every inch of my heart. I also thank my brothers and sisters for being exceptional siblings. Even when we have family disputes, we never stop loving each other (Bryant, Greg, Audrey, Vanessa, Maurice and Stevie). To my nieces and nephews, I love you with all of my heart. To my friends who have never left my side, thank you (Tiffany, Tenkya, Janine, Jessica, Carla, Cara, Cassandra, Deborah, Michelle, Rhea, April, Patrice, Tammy B., Lauri P., and the P.U.M.P.S. (Providing U Motivation to Pursue Success) Board Members Eboni M., Kelly M., and Tammy D.).

I thank my aunts, uncles, cousins, close associates, and God children for their unconditional love. Special thanks goes to Lissa Woodson for her expertise on writing books, Johnathan Swain, Scot Scott of Biohertz, William Stokes and the modeling team that helped me develop all the details on the cover of the book.

I thank my clients for their continuous support, everyone that I thanked in Dare to Walk in My Shoes, I send the same message out of appreciation for your support.

The difference between what we do, and what we are capable of doing, would solve most of the world's problems.

---Mahatma Gandhi

From My Heart to Yours…

Life is waiting on you

What kind of shoe would you consider yourself to be? I used to be a loafer and was stepped all over in most cases. Now I'm a die-hard stiletto, turning heads and making progressive moves that are bringing about amazing changes in my life. Have you looked down at your feet lately to see what you're wearing? Have you ever thought about why you chose that shoe to go with that outfit on that day?

Every morning I crank up my favorite song at the time, stand in front of my big, rustic, life-sized mirror and sing and dance as if no one will ever see or hear me. I then plow through my walk-in closet and go through my shoes. I decide what type of mood I'm in and based upon that decide which shoe will best complement that mood. If I'm feeling sexy, I throw on my 4-inch, leopard print stilettos. If I'm feeling classic I may choose a modest-heeled, round-toed pump. On those days when I'd rather stay in bed than get out and handle my business, I may go for a fun, furry boot. You get it; my mood and my shoes go hand-in-hand.

Do you believe that a simple pair of shoes can change the way you feel? When I place on a banging pair of boots, I feel like I'm on top of the world. When a pair of strappy sandals meets my feet, I feel adorably sexy and powerful. The shoes I choose matter to me and will soon matter to you.

The same power that existed in Dorothy from the Wizard of Oz when she slid on her red, shiny PUMPS can also exist in you. Let's step into a new life together, because the world is waiting on the footprints we will leave as we achieve greatness. Hear my story: the trials and triumphs. Witness how the power of stepping tall in the shoes designed for you can completely change your life.

The oversized gold-framed mirror installed in the shoe salon was a major part of a pink, bubble gum fantasy. I wanted my clientele to look in that mirror and reconnect with their childhood and wanted the women who strolled into the store to feel pampered and pretty—like princesses.

However, there were many days I looked in the mirror and saw the "ugly" unspoken truth in its reflection. When my clients and staff looked at me, they saw a successful businesswoman. They saw a friend. They saw a smile—always. But I could never fool the mirror. My smile didn't quite reach my eyes any more. How could it? The business was losing money faster than high heels could break under pressure. My real estate investments were costing more money than they gained. The strain of trying to maintain appearances was slowly sucking the life out of me.

The mirror knew it all.

When I reached the lowest point ... the point of no return, the point of not caring anymore, something wonderful happened. *Vision.*

From this vision I was able to cut losses, refocus my life's strategy and build a circle of power that would set everything back on track. From this vision, I gathered the strength and discipline to turn it all around. No longer am I just looking the part of a successful woman—I am now living it. Thanks to a few key changes in my life, the mirror now holds a new image—one of a refined, young woman with a new vivacious attitude on life.

I invite you to take a walk in a new pair of shoes,

get a glimpse of my life—the mistakes, the indecisions, and most of all, the victories. It is my hope that by the end of this book you, too, will stand tall on a solid life strategy that will revolutionize your personal outlook and re-energize your inner being. This journey will help change your thoughts and your actions. Prosperity and happiness are only a few steps away.

Are you with me? Alright then.

Let's step!

Power of CHANGE
In Shoes

Life brings about many unexpected changes. Imagine waking up in the morning. You shower, brush your hair, put on your favorite outfit and off you go to school, work or to run errands. The weather outside is perfect. Not a cloud in the sky. Your day couldn't get any better. Then the unthinkable happens. Your vehicle is hit head-on by an oncoming driver. Your outfit is now dirty and torn. Your hair, well, the nurses shave it off on one side in order to make an incision to address your swelling head. Material things no longer matter. You are now teetering on the line between life and death.

What thoughts race through your mind? You may try to remember the last words you said to your loved ones. You may reflect on your life and prior conversations and incidents. Was that argument you had with your mother REALLY worth it? Did you apologize to your sister for calling her out of her name? Did you tell your best friend you were sorry for ditching her to go kick it with your boyfriend? What will people say about you at your funeral? And most of all, what do you regret?

As you lay on the operating table your heart is pounding so hard you can feel its beat in your throat. You're more conscious of each breath you take now, as you don't know which one could be your last. Are you thinking about that vision you had for your life? You know, the one you constantly put off because you were afraid to take that first step.   You always said, I'll start it the first of next month. Now, here it is the 28th of the month after that goal, and your guaranteed ticket to experience life on the 1st isn't as reliable as you hoped.

Who told you to take life for granted like this? Breathe…Breathe…the last breath of life…within a blink of an eye it's all over. Life is non-existent and your chances to change are gone…Let's take our thoughts back to the reality of today: this very moment. Breathe, Breathe…yes, you are still alive. You are still breathing and have an opportunity to make a great difference in your life. Don't take tomorrow for granted… live and bask in today's moment. Today's opportunities. Follow the desires of your heart…fulfill your dreams…Life waits for no one…you are no exception to this rule. (Exercise the Power to CHANGE)

Chapter 1

Mary Janes
Small Steps to Great Victory

Allow me, for a moment, to take the time to recall this most painful chapter of my life. Life is not easy, so I plan to, as *Sister 2 Sister* magazine, says, "give it to you straight, no chaser".

Entering the new world of positive thinking with true understanding of self is vital, because *YOU* are the foundation of your life, of your empire. Empires built upon shaky foundations or with unknown substances are destined to collapse.

Some have asked why I decided to open a shoe salon. What lies behind this passion for pumps? On the one foot, I have a shoe fetish that I want to share with the world, and on the other, a passion for pampering and empowering women. I want to adorn their feet with fancy shoes. What many don't realize is this passion, this love, is the result of several painful experiences in my own life.

Consider this: when standing tall, shoes are the farthest things from the natural eye. Though the eyes are the windows to the soul, there are ways to draw attention away from the place where everyone seems to first look. The prettier the shoes, the less likely one is to focus on the eyes—and especially the secrets, pain, disappointment or hurt that may dwell behind them. Herein lies where my story begins and the truth unfolds.

I grew up on the South Side of Chicago—in Auburn-Gresham—not too far from the Englewood area. I humbly confess that I lived in a two-parent home and am grateful for the opportunity I had growing up to witness what love could be like between two married individuals. It also gave me the ability to see the ups and downs relationships often experience. Through it all, for the love of their six children, my parents were able to press through their difficulties and provide a decent life for us.

My father, the backbone of the Johnson family, had only a third grade education. I smile every time I think about this, because growing up I never realized how uneducated my father was. In fact, I knew very little about my father's educational history until my early 20s. My daddy made sure we were everywhere the name of Jesus was mentioned: Wednesday night Bible study, Thursday evening Bible class at home, Friday choir practice at church—even though I couldn't sing the right note to save my life—and Sunday we would be at every church service, morning, noon and night. When I saw my father in any educational capacity, it was with his Bible in hand. I would hear him read one of those sixty-six books all the time. Naturally, he stumbled over many of the words, but so did I. I never questioned how smart my dad was and didn't have to. He was an awesome provider and businessman. That's all I needed to know.

My mother graduated from high school and went on to become a cashier, so there wasn't a very heavy emphasis on education in my household. My father, on the other hand, was very adamant in making sure that I, as well as my five siblings, understood the principles and benefits of entrepreneurship. In more ways than one, that was a blessing in my life; though I will tell anyone that having both—education and drive to become an entrepreneur—are keys to achieving immeasurable success.

My father, even with only a third grade education, owned multiple businesses including a limousine company that rented cars to funeral homes. He even contracted his limos out to the ever-famous Leak Funeral Home, presently run by Spencer Leak, Jr. and family. He also owned a liquor store, record store and many other small businesses. It amazes me, even to this day, that my father could not read, but one thing he could do was count and keep up with his money. When I was about 12 years old, he told me that as a young Black woman I may find it hard in life to work for other people, and that at some point someone would be in control of how much money I made and how far I could go. He told me that I needed to be an "entroproknow." (Yes, he said it exactly that way).

I fondly remember the day my 5th grade teacher at Clara Barton Elementary school, Mrs. Latham, asked me what I wanted to be when I grew up.

I pushed back my chair, stood up before my class, and said proudly, "I want to be an 'entroproknow' just like my dad."

Mrs. Latham grinned; my peers laughed. I wasn't embarrassed. They didn't know the admiration I had for my father and couldn't possibly understand the concept of having your own business. Mrs. Latham took the time to explain entrepreneurism to me and also taught me its proper pronunciation. Fortunately, she didn't discourage me, as so many others do when children aspire to do something outside the norm. When I was a child, black people landed desk jobs with average or below average salaries. Only a few became doctors, lawyers, or journalists. No one else in my class desired to achieve the same goals as I did. Somehow it didn't deter me or make me feel ashamed of my choice. If my father could do it, then so could I, a little black girl from the South Side of Chicago.

Though my father worked many hours a day away from home, when he was in our presence, he always talked about what he did for a living. He loved all of his jobs, and loved being his own boss. I soaked up his love for that kind of freedom as though they were my daily lessons. My siblings eventually went into fields that were as far away from being business owners as possible. I think my father's zeal and his drive for business rubbed off on me with every conversation and every answered question——and, believe me, I had many.

My mother, however, was the total opposite of my father. She simply wanted to be comfortable. She supported her husband and children. My mom put her dreams on hold to make sure her kids had a good life. She supported me through college and never left my side. There was an abundance of potential inside of my mother, but she let life drag along and missed out on the opportunity to achieve her higher calling. My mom and dad have been married for over 50 years and they made it work to provide for their family and I love them for persevering through tough times together.

My father, a very frugal man, didn't believe in wasting money or resources. We were his "human" resources—especially since he put food on the table, clothes on our backs, and a roof over our heads. Each one of his children spent time working in his business in one capacity or another. I like to say that we were little "Jamaicans" (three job mon!), which is not a slight in any way as Jamaicans are generally known to be hard-working and extremely enterprising. The job I hated most was the limousine service. When the cars were dirty, we had to whip out the soap and towels, hose them and sponge wash until they were sparkling clean. That was fine for summer, but as everyone knows, Chicago winters can be brutal. We were outside in below zero temperatures washing, drying, shining, waxing or whatever. I felt like Karate Kid, "Wax On, Wax Off." It's no wonder I have a great love for warm clothing, forced air heating, and a sheer infatuation with furry boots. They all serve as good armor against the Chicago 'hawk' we faced while on my father's clock.

Our jobs outside the home did not overshadow what we were required to do in the kitchen, bathrooms and garden in our little Cape Cod house on Seeley Avenue. I can remember once being awakened at one o'clock in the morning with my father yelling at the top of his lungs. When he would yell, I was instantly like a soldier standing at attention, because it was usually butt-whipping time. All I could think is, "Jesus, what did we do wrong this time?" He woke everyone in the house, made us come downstairs, and told us to line up in front of his bed before pointing to the mussed covers.

"Why didn't y'all make up my bed?"

This was something so simple, but it mattered to him, especially since my mother was pulling the late-night shift as a cashier. All six of us got a little whipping that morning before being sent back to bed. Trust me! His bed was made every day after that. Chores around the house—painting the garage, gardening, doing dishes, laundry, cooking (at age 12 for me which I didn't perfect until I was 34)—were taken as seriously as the jobs we had working for our dad. Slacking was strictly prohibited in either case.   And I certainly took him and any responsibilities I was given very seriously. Sometimes, maybe too seriously. I stopped eating cereal and playing with dolls at nine years old. I thought both were quite childish, and in no way did I want to be considered a child, especially since I aspired to be an "entroproknow" just like my dad.

During my childhood my world revolved around the community, and the community revolved around the church. Everyone loved my father. He was serious, business-oriented, hardworking, funny, reliable, honest and trustworthy, but he didn't play. The few times he smiled were from jokes he told himself or from being around his family, including his sisters and brothers. I learned a great deal from him. My father introduced me to God, and exposed me to the world of managing and owning a business, but there was one thing missing. He never really showed me that he loved me. I longed for him to hug me or tell me that I was daddy's little girl, because that's what I saw happening in the lives of neighborhood children when they interacted with their fathers.

I learned later in life that my father's parents weren't very affectionate. He couldn't do something for me that hadn't been shown or given to him. Wanting and desiring to feel special in the eyes of my father led to me making many mistakes in life when it came to men. This resulted in painful moments in my childhood and experiences in my teen years that weighed heavily on every aspect of my life and were carried into my adulthood.

In high school, I was a different type of young lady. I entered into a long-term relationship at a very early age—15 to be specific. My boyfriend at the time was raised in a Catholic household with a strict upbringing. His parents were not receptive to "outsiders," but I made it into their tight circle for a while. Unfortunately, that soon changed when his parents could no longer stand the sight of me. In their eyes, I was taking their young boy and turning him into a man way too soon. This was heartbreaking as a teenager, but I later learned that teenagers often mistake lust for love which leads to many pains and problems in the future.

My boyfriend and I dated until I turned 21. Being in a relationship at such an early age caused me to gravitate and cling to what I thought was love, because I was trying to fill the void my father left. At least I perceived it to be a void. Unlike some households, at least my dad was there and provided for us, but a great deal of the time I missed him due to the long hours he spent working hard to provide for us. I would later learn that "time" is just one of the sacrifices that are made when you decide to be an entrepreneur.

When you are trying to find love, you will mistake anything for that coveted interaction. I mistook infatuation for love. Looking back I can admit that being in a "serious" relationship at such an early age is detrimental to the mental health of a young woman or man. Although it doesn't feel that way at the time, the relationship becomes a distraction from educational goals and reaching the next level in life. It's a hindrance to developing healthy relationships with others since everything and every action of every day becomes filtered through the eyes of your partner. Instead of relying on one's inner voice, the spirit of God that dwells in each one of us, approval is sought from that other person before moving in a direction that one knows is right.

Like so many teenagers who had walked into "love," I began to lose my identity. Many things have been put in place to ensure that young men and women have the boundaries and a frame of character reference to draw from: the Bible, church, sports, dance and reading. Regrettably, I stepped totally outside of those things while trying to be my own "little woman." That in itself was one of the biggest mistakes I have ever made. Having control over one's own person, one's life, is the key to a strong foundation.

When I was in high school I thought I was a business woman. I carried a briefcase instead of a book bag, wore heels instead of gym shoes, and dressed in silk blouses and skirts instead of trousers and sweats. I was not the type of young lady to attend games or other school functions, because I thought they were childish. I was very popular in school and not the type of person to get in trouble. I just thought I was "grown." Looking back, I realize I missed out on a lot of fun things—things that would have shaped my experiences much differently. My actions stemmed from being in a relationship where I wanted to be taken seriously. I wanted him to love and desire me and sought to separate myself from the other girls. I wasn't like them and wanted him to know and acknowledge that fact. I was an overachiever with above-average grades, but they would have been stellar if I wasn't trying so hard to impress "Mr. Man."

Some of the mistakes I made then affected my life years later. When I went away to college, I plunged feet first into credit card debt traveling back and forth from Normal, Illinois to Chicago every weekend to be with him. I had 14 credit cards and four gas station cards (mind you, I didn't have a car). After two years in college, they were all maxed out. Bill collectors were ringing my phone 24/7. I had to work long hours to pay off the credit cards. I was tired. I was exhausted. I was distracted. My grades started to fall. I gave up and ran back home to be with him. He was my comfort and my security. I felt like Beyonce' when she sang about being "Crazy In Love." I was so out of character. I lost my scholarship and with it went my integrity. I damn near lost my mind.

I practically made a fool of myself when I found out that I, the woman who had given up so much for "love," was merely a speck of female dust on his "Player" radar. The weekend before Labor Day we stayed at his friend's home for the weekend. It was the middle of the night. We were all asleep. The phone began to ring. My first thought was to assume it was his friend calling to check on us. Inwardly, unfortunately, I knew that was far from the case. So, I got up to answer the phone.

I calmly picked up the receiver and said, "Hello."

A woman responded with nothing more than a breathy, "Hello."

I stilled myself because my gut was telling me something just wasn't right. I kept my cool. No need to jump to conclusions, right?

I said, "Hi, how are you? Who would you like to speak to?"

She said, "Keith."

My heart fell down to my toes. I couldn't reel in my emotions. Simply put, I was pissed, so I screamed, "Who is this?"

She simply said, "This is Jackie. Who are *you*?" As if she had a right to demand anything.

I retorted, "Jackie who? And why are you calling here, at this house, for my man?"

Then she replied with the words every woman dreads. "Baby, I was there with him yesterday."

I woke Keith. Not with words though. No, I was furious. So, I took the telephone and slammed it against his head. As he was frightened out of a sound sleep, I dropped that tiny bit of information about Jackie into his ear. He immediately started with lies and back-peddling. He said I was crazy, that he didn't know who that was and someone was trying to frame him. Lies—all of it. And the sad part is that I started to believe him anyway. I pictured the last six years: the times I missed my high school football games to be in his company; blew off my friends and my family; put him before everyone; loved him more than I loved myself; and sought his approval for my life. I thought of all these times and realized I invested too much of myself. To walk away at this point would mean I did it all for nothing.

Although I knew I wouldn't go too far, I pretended I was about to leave him to force his hand on professing his love for me or some kind of reaction from him other than just the lies spewing from his lips. When I made it to the elevator, two ladies were getting off——one of them was three times my petite size, and the other was just my size.

She quickly sized me up and said, "You must be Nicky."

I could only reply with, "You must be Jackie."

As she nodded, I said, "Let's knock on this door and figure out what's going on."

When Keith pulled open the door and saw the three of us, he almost passed out. Then the fight began. She screamed at him. I screamed at him. And her friend put in her little two cents, too. I kept my eye on the big girl because she looked a lot like the terminator! While Jackie screamed at him, I thought of survival and wondered how I could take her down! Overall, it was not a pleasant undertaking. We woke everyone on that floor of that high rise building in South Shore.

Now here's the sad part, I was so bold at the time and so filled with what I believed was love that I was going to fight for "my man." I grabbed the bat from a nearby closet and stormed toward the front door. The ladies weren't really trying to deal with anything going upside their heads, so they swiftly moved toward the elevators. After I watched Jackie cry and cry and plead for him to be with her, he told her she was crazy and shut the door in her face. And somehow I thought I had won the prize. Little did I know, I lost much more than I gained. I was now an official card-carrying member of the low self-esteem club. This was merely the beginning of a roller coaster ride of painful relationships. Jackie was deceived by Keith just like I had been, yet I wanted to "Freddie Krueger" her even more than I wanted to hurt him.

Young teenage women and men must learn to respect each other's boundaries and understand the importance of having healthy, productive relationships. Your main focus should be your future success. Relationships will come and go, but you will never get back your youth. Homecomings, football games, parties, nights at the show with your girls, and hanging out with your boys are the times worth enjoying. Take this time to explore an internship with a company that interests you, find a part-time job to work while completing your school studies, and actively participate in extra curricular activities.

There is something inside of you that is secretly waiting to surface; let it begin to live and breathe. The dreams and visions you have can and will manifest if you put time, energy and effort into them. Yes, you are young, but don't waste this precious time of life. Build your talents; develop your skills, walking boldly before any opportunity to gain more knowledge. Invest in yourself so that you can reap a huge return. Most teenage relationships do not last. That is one reason they are called "puppy love." Yes, enjoy being a teenager and have uncommitted conversations and occasional movie dates, but utilize this time right now…this crucial time…to endow into yourself. Build your self-image and self-esteem, work on productive projects, and see how quickly multiple doors open for you.

Be Who You Were Designed to Be…Be Not Afraid.

I've always wanted to become an entrepreneur. Being an entrepreneur isn't an idea one pulls out of thin air. There must be a driving, passionate force that completely ignites your inner being. People that seek to become entrepreneurs strictly because they don't want to take orders from another person are doing it for the wrong reasons. Entrepreneurs are witty, strong-willed, determined, and most importantly, they must be in it for the long haul.

As a child, I was motivated by my father's determination to succeed. I admired him more as a young adult when I realized he succeeded with only a third grade education. Now there are many opportunities to receive education and training. Before deciding to pursue business ownership, know exactly what you want to be and understand your reasons. Prior to becoming a business owner, I had a zeal for setting my own schedule, creating my dream salary, and building an empire in my community for everyone to enjoy. My initial thoughts of being an entrepreneur as a child, teenager, and adult were all completely different than what I was actually faced with in the real world. However, they were based on watching my father's experiences and learning about entrepreneurship.

Wikipedia states that an entrepreneur "is a person that has possession of an enterprise and venture and assumes significant accountability for the inherent risks and the outcome. It is an ambitious leader who combines land, labor and capital to often create and market new goods or services." Key words are stated here...*a person assuming risk and outcomes.* This is more than a person with a great vision. Know that entrepreneurship is the right direction for your life, because the decision to build a business without the commitment can be a costly, timely and disappointing venture. I encourage people to own their own business because the entrepreneurial spirit lives and breathes inside of them, the desire fills their thoughts and dreams, and they are prepared to dedicate their lives to that mission.

This is my passion, but what is yours? Let's devise a plan for you to begin the process, understand available career choices, and learn necessary skills to increase success. If you believe that being a doctor sounds interesting...you must go to your community hospital and find out how to shadow with doctors for a day to see their work and how it is accomplished. No more sitting around playing Wii, Xbox, texting friends, Facebooking or getting into unnecessary trouble. Instead of wasting valuable time, exercise your mind to prepare for greatness.

Chapter 1 : Ponder over these questions

What is stopping you from stepping out of your comfort zone right now to achieve the big dream that permeates or infiltrates your thoughts daily?

Get out your journal and write out your thoughts.

"There is more in us than we know. If we can be made to see it, perhaps, for the rest of our lives, we will be unwilling to settle for less."   *- Kurt Hahn*

Chapter 2

Sling Backs

Take a second look back.

You're farther than where you came from

What is holding you back from the desires of your heart? Is it that you don't believe in them? Is your self-confidence down, and you are not sure that you can't accomplish the task? Imagine a life filled with the desires of your heart. Imagine a home--that could simply be comfortable with Crate and Barrel accents in every room and a black iron gate outside, or even a home like some of the ones shown on MTV Cribs. Guess what? These are your thoughts. Think BIG or small…your choice, but be true to yourself and allow it to be something that you really desire. Now, picture yourself riding in the car that you desire…is it a Pinto? Oops! I'm not sure if they even make that type of car any more… or is it a Porshe? These are your dreams and your thoughts. Make them the way you want. Can you see your dreams clearly? Can you feel your dreams? Do they feel real? Close your eyes tightly and imagine yourself in that home or driving that fancy car with an abundance of money in the bank. Ok, open your eyes now and let reality sink in.

If you desire the finer things in life, you must WORK for them. They are obtainable and within your reach, if you put in your time, energy, and strong efforts. Take the limits off your thinking. Stop saying, "I can't acquire good grades", "I hate that teacher", "My parents make you sick", "The world is mistreating me", and the infamous, "The teacher doesn't like me". Are you truly giving everything that you have to be successful? Or, are you playing the game waiting or expecting for some miracle to come and change your situation? You are the miracle, and the drive is deep inside of you. Get ready to put the car in drive! Take it out of park and get busy living a refined life. Let's talk; it's time to be honest with yourself. Do you fear failing? Are you afraid of change? The only way you can improve is by accepting the truth, regardless of how ugly it may be. Accepting it will open up a door that no man can shut…but you.

If you desire something different, you must do something different. Let me tell you how to be a "Dream Chaser" and turn your life around.

Life is everything you chose to make it

My father laid the foundation, but over time I acquired the taste and the drive to know what it was like to become my own boss. Then I learned from a mistake my father had made. He had not shared the wisdom of proper planning and saving money. He knew how to make it, but not how to save for a rainy day . . . or any day for that matter.

Let's do the math. My father had multiple business, didn't know how to save or plan ahead, and had several mouths to feed and to provide for—so with everything coming in—there was much more going out. By most people's definition, we were still working-class poor. I felt I was destined to live a better quality of life, but the $20,000 debt I accumulated during those two years of college soon had me living in the style that I grew up in and sometimes not even that.

Since I thought I was "grown" and no longer wanted advice from my parents, I had moved out and lived in poor conditions. Everything coming in was already designated to go right back out and none of my income was used for the things I wanted to do. Like father, like daughter. I wish my family—or someone—would have told me the dangers of too much credit and not using it wisely. It would have prevented many years of financial hardship. I started in the negative rather than hitting the ground running from zero and going upward and onward from that point.

That $20,000 worth of debt felt like $200,000. My ignorance forced me to take jobs that did not require a strong educational background and often included manual labor. I landed a job as 10-key punch operator at Northern Trust Bank, a Fortune 500 company. Trust me that "Fortune" didn't end up in my bank account. Let me explain what this job entailed. As people withdrew and deposited funds for their accounts, I was the one responsible for imputing the little black numbers on the bottom of the check that identify the dollar amount of each check.

The job was initially a temporary position, and I would have to prove myself to stay in a more permanent capacity. I worked from 5:00 a.m. to 8:00 a.m.—a mere three hours every day, which meant working two other jobs just to make ends meet. I was attracted to a higher standard of living though I didn't have it growing up. I

wanted fancy cars, designer suits, money, and power—
things that seemed to command respect. One major
reason I desired these things could be traced back to
my self-esteem issues—the need for approval, the need
for love, the need for someone or something outside of
myself to say that I was valuable. I felt that if I could
look good on the outside, people would assume that
everything on the inside mirrored the same.

At the age of 21, when all my friends were graduating
from college, beginning wonderful corporate careers,
going on vacations, and enjoying life, I was climbing my
way out of debt and trying to regain stability.

A manager at The Northern Trust Company (TNT)
by the name of Greg Barber walked up to me one night
and said, "You don't belong here. Why are you here?"

Classic question. I looked at him and couldn't
respond, because my mind went blank. He said, "take a
look around." For the first time after a year of being in
that place, I noticed my co-workers. All of them were
middle-aged, mostly black women, with families—some
with grandchildren—with very little income. But what
stood out most on their faces and posture were sad and
serious expressions. Most of them were unhappy. This
is where my life was headed.

That evening we engaged in a long conversation one
that I will never forget. Greg, having taken the time to
point out the obvious, sparked fear in my soul. I didn't
want to still punch numbers 30 years from that moment.
I didn't want to settle for less. It would be different if the
women were happy and if this was their career choice.
For the most part, it was all they could do because of
their education or lack thereof; it was also due to the fact
that they didn't necessarily aspire to do more than collect
a paycheck at a job that was far beneath their abilities.
Though there is nothing wrong with that if it makes you

happy, it wasn't for me—and I'm sure that given another opportunity—it really wasn't for them either.

Most of us desire to do something different, something great. It is fear that keeps us stuck in places we really don't want to be. It is a lack of choices or fear of failure that stifles us. Those women, my co-workers, reminded me of my mother—the fact that she "tolerated" my father's aspirations. Sadly, deep in her heart, she also settled. She worked as a cashier at a liquor store for several years until it closed with minimum pay and not many opportunities for advancement. She wasn't happy either.

This revelation and reflection proved to be an awakening for me. I got my butt back in school—pronto. Attending Malcolm X College, a community college, only added to my already hectic schedule, but living with the stigma of being a college dropout was not an option. Not one member of my immediate family had a college education, and I wanted to be different. No one in my immediate family encouraged my desire to finish college. I had to cheer for myself and find ways to position myself around other positive influences.

Greg told me that since I was over 21, investing my money would be the smart way to go. My question to him was, "What money?" I still hadn't cleared the debt by any stretch of the imagination. And like many around me, I was living paycheck to paycheck. There were days when even the bare necessities escaped my reach. But I didn't brush off his advice, either. I tucked it into a small corner of my mind knowing that the moment any extra money surfaced, I would invest it. In the meantime, I would learn what I could about investing.

Greg also inspired me to find a better job within the company. I was actually beginning to believe that the job I held was all I could have—that I had messed up so badly there was no way out. I soon learned a lesson about life and about faith: there is always a window of opportunity waiting to be opened and waiting to pour in sunshine. Greg cracked open the window with just a few words that night. My drive and initiative did the rest. I took a job in the vault to get off the night shift so I would be able to meet more people within corporate America. Lifting 70 lb bags of other people's money meant I could at least be surrounded by what rich folks took for granted every day——an unending supply of cash. The Northern Trust Company was the place where the ultra rich put their money . . . money in established trust funds, corporations, and multi-million dollar empires. Thankfully, this job did not require me to dress professionally. Unlike my high school years of wearing business casual clothing and carrying a briefcase, I couldn't afford to buy a scarf, let alone a suit although I always snuck in a pair of cute, affordable shoes ... no matter what.

After three months of building my muscles by lifting those heavy bags, my back went out. I weighed a buck-o-five soaking wet, and some of those bags were bigger than my petite frame. Now I was caught in another dilemma: find another job within the company in thirty days or I would have to leave altogether. As my blessings always seem to amaze me, a lady by the name of Islee Ferguson, who has since made her earthly transition, provided me with an opportunity of a lifetime. Though I had no experience in that area, she offered the opportunity for a client service position, which is as far from vault work as one could get. On the day of the interview, I purchased a red dress from the thrift store and walked in with that old high school briefcase to add to the "look" and "feel" of the position. Little did I know, red was not the best color to wear in a banking environment—especially since it was layered on a dress that hugged every curve I had (and ones I didn't know about). Fortunately, Islee saw past the dress, but lovingly suggested that I invest in "other clothes."

When Mrs. Ferguson asked about my work experience during the interview, I thought that honesty was the best policy. I answered her with a simple, "Ms. Ferguson, everyone else that you might interview can walk in this door and tell you that they've had years of experience servicing clients. I cannot."

As she took a deep breath, I continued speaking, "However, the one thing that is important, is that they know how to do it *their* way, and I'm going to do it *exactly* the way you teach me, with a fresh start and with no preconceived notions about how it should be done. That in itself gives me a competitive edge."

Needless to say, she loved my tenacity and agreed to give me a chance. This was nothing short of a miracle . . . at least in my eyes! As a client service associate, I did every single thing it took to learn all aspects of the banking business. I brought the prospectus home and studied it as well as the Scriptures my father made us study in the Bible. I tried my best to know the answers to questions that investors would even *think* to ask. I arrived to work early every day and stayed well past closing time. Anytime someone was needed to work overtime, I volunteered! I became known as someone who was dependable, trustworthy, honest, and went above and beyond the call of duty.

Sound familiar? Like father, like daughter.

Over time, I inspired other employees with motivational and encouraging words. Strangely enough, I ended up teaching people who had been there for years things about the business that they never took the time to read or comprehend. This was about the time I noticed that some people didn't value their jobs or the opportunities they had been given and it was a shame. There I was, coming from a position where I punched numbers on checks, to a point of back-breaking work inside the vault, then to a position that exposed me to a variety of people requiring the use of perception, brains and tenacity, and it was taken for granted by some of those around me.

After one year in that position, I received an impressive raise——which I certainly appreciated. Then a very confusing situation occurred. A workflow coordinator's position became available, and I just knew that job was for me. I *knew* Mrs. Ferguson was going to give that job to me, especially since I was practically handling all aspects of the position anyway. I was brought into a meeting with the certainty that the position was all but mine. To my surprise, each person in my unit was introduced to our "new" workflow coordinator—— someone who didn't have a stitch of experience! Now how did that happen? I worked my sling back pumps off (and a few other things, too), and this man, dressed in a suit (with fine-looking shoes might I add), walked in and just took *my* position. I was completely dismayed.

Where did he come from?

What made them think he was better suited for the position?

A few days later, I built up the courage to walk into Mrs. Ferguson's office to request a meeting.

Through my tears I managed to ask, "How could you do this to me?"

Looking back, I realize I was much too emotional. However, this beautiful, dark-skinned, robust woman looked at me as if to say, "Do what?" And if I remember correctly, she said those exact words.

I dried my tears before continuing. "How could you

let that man take *my* job? I have worked my toes to the nub."

She leaned back in her big black office chair. "Nicole, yes. You would deserve this job, but when were you going to tell me that's what you wanted to do? Am I supposed to *guess* that you want to be a manager? During your performance appraisals, did you mention your career goals or your desire to go into management?"

She leaned forward, looking me straight in the eyes as her voice became solid and steady and said, "If you want something in life, you'd better learn to ask for it." I didn't blink an eye as I processed the words and lesson coming from her mouth. I dried what was left of my tears, squared my shoulders, and in the strongest voice I could manage, said, "I want to go into management. Now what do I need to do to get there?"

She smiled at me and answered simply, "Keep doing what you're doing."

I continued to work even harder. Two months later, a team leader position became available—one that was above the work flow coordinator. The job was handed to me in a silver slipper—with a nice raise, too! The woman didn't have to tell me twice! Ask and it shall be given. Another lesson learned from just one of the wonderful people I met on my life's journey.

Are you giving school your full potential? Are you taking time to increase exposure for yourself by working internships and having a job? How are you investing your time right now?

Accepting minimalism for your grades and work habits is completely UNACCEPTABLE. Your future is directly tied to your efforts today.

Stop speaking words of defeat over yourself such as, "I'm never going to pass this class. It's too hard. The teacher doesn't like me, etc, etc, etc." Instead begin to speak victoriously. "I will turn this C into an A." Affirm goodness back into your life by becoming your own motivator and encourager. Stop settling for less and believing you will just get by. Getting by does not allow you the opportunity to get ahead. Begin to have thoughts of increase and aim for MORE. Believe in yourself and surround yourself with others that believe in you too!

Chapter 2:Ponder over these questions

What do you absolutely love to do? Why? How will you begin to achieve these goals going forward? Write an action plan to improve your grades and work habits.

Write your thoughts in your journal.

"Reach out and open the door that no one thought could be opened. Life is behind it."

- Kelly Ann Rothaus

A Good life is not lived by Chance but by Choice. - Kobi Yamada

CHAPTER 3

STEP FIRMLY. YOU MADE A DECISION TO CHANGE.
IT'S NOT EASY…BUT IT'S POSSIBLE

"To whom much is given much is required." This famous Bible quote is as true as they come. Let me ask you a question. Do you think you will have good grades without studying? How will you make the team or get the acting job when you haven't even practiced or rehearsed? Even the best of them (Denzel Washington, Kobe Bryant, Trey Songz, etc.) have to practice to reach perfection. You are no different. No, it's not easy…stop the pity party…stop crying and most of all stop making excuses. It's time to make new decisions for yourself and your own life.

I'm not down-playing your situation. It may be very difficult. Your parents may be on drugs, you may live in an apartment with no lights, or maybe your loved one has passed on and you feel alone. I know it's hard, but instead of placing focus on the problems, focus on the future. "There's nothing new under the sun"; other people have been where you are. If they can make it, so can you. You can't let the troubles of life get you so far down that you begin to have a personal relationship with failure. Remove yourself from the negative state that is capturing your thoughts and stealing your joy. It is time, time for TRUE CHANGE.

I met some students that come from great homes, have phenomenal parents and receive everything with a silver spoon, yet they appreciate nothing. They have no clue of the everyday struggles many of us face to survive. Many times they take all of their possessions and love for granted. Their lives are pretty on the outside, but their attitude towards their blessings is ugly. Is this you? Are you really happy? If not, isn't it time for change? Let's do it!

Everyone has a story. You may not understand why is it imperative to think positively and restore gratefulness to your heart. However, it is important to try and grasp these concepts before it is too late. Do you have the courage to put forth the effort to achieve true change? Here is my story.

Stand firm in your decision to put forth change

The Northern Trust Company position was working out fine, but because I still had a mountain of debt facing me, I also worked another job as a leasing agent. This time in my life reminded me a great deal of my childhood days when I, along with my siblings, worked at several of my father's businesses. Same work ethic, different time.

As a leasing agent, I had the opportunity to meet another person who would make a dynamic impact on my life. Lessons learned while listening to Greg Barber at TNT became useful during my time at the leasing office.

Greg had already encouraged me to invest five percent of my paycheck into stocks. For a number of reasons I felt I could not afford to do it. I barely had anything to buy food once all my bills were paid, but he said I couldn't afford *not* to do it. I decided to take his challenge and found a way to invest something out of every check. The amounts were so small that when I received the quarterly statements, I just filed them away. After about a year, I noticed the amount of funds I had available had actually doubled! My first inclination was to withdraw it all, baby! Instead I increased the amount of money I was investing from five percent to eight percent. Now even more sacrifices had to be made on the home front, such as visits to the hair stylist only taking place once a month. Eventually, I ended up doing my own hair and nails and even went on a complete strike from clothes and jewelry shopping. However, I would treat myself to one thing on occasion—shoes to accent my wardrobe, to liven things up—but no other luxuries were allowed.

Buckling down also meant that eating out was

completely out of the question. Unfortunately, at the time I didn't know how to cook that well. Though my father taught me how to cook some things, I ended up buying and stocking up on canned goods to stay well fed. This was a very humbling experience for me. As my investments continued to grow, I wasn't hurting or upset (though I did get sick of the food I could actually cook, like spaghetti). I was happy to make sacrifices that would make my life better.

There are certain things I have considered to be my greatest attributes——having an open mind and the willingness to listen and learn, especially from people who have demonstrated great leadership. I believe you can learn something from anyone; even if it's how you *don't* want to be like that person or mirror their actions.

For instance, I used to work out in the gym every morning at TNT. But even after leaving the gym, I would scarf down a Snickers bar, which was counterproductive. When I first started working out, there was this attractive, well-built trainer with blonde hair and blue eyes. Studying him and examining how he did things led me to believe that he was a prime example of leadership when it came to working out. He shared successful techniques, his eating habits and all the essential things that I needed to know to build and strengthen my body.

He left the company a couple of years later and was replaced by a beautiful, friendly, wonderful young woman. Unfortunately, she didn't practice any of the things she tried to teach. By comparison to my previous trainer, this woman was shorter than my 5'5" frame and over 200 pounds. Her appearance and lack of discipline soon resulted in my inability to work out with her. Not that I was judging her harshly, but I, like so many others, expect a leader to lead by example. She and I did have one thing in common: we loved Snickers. Nevertheless, if you're going to teach people, you should learn and apply it to your own life first. For example, Greg Barber knew how and what to do with investing in the stock market. Greg's sound advice helped me in my next financial undertaking, but it was the example from the young, female trainer that would make me take a long, hard look at my personal values.

Cleveland McCowan, property manager for a new development project in Chicago, introduced me to the wonderful world of real estate right in the community where I currently reside. Now full circle, I'm back in the booming Bronzeville area. Not only did Cleveland introduce me to the real estate world, he taught me how to be a great businesswoman. Although I didn't have any leasing experience when I applied for the job, I used my famous line——the same one that landed me the customer service position at TNT: *Hey they already know what to do, but I'm going to do it the way you teach me——and to perfection.*

Now I was 22 years old, had been investing for one year and was still living check to check. Ultimately, I would carve a way out. As I listened to and mirrored other successful people, I learned and grew beyond measure.

One day Cleveland said something to me I knew, for sure, was a joke. "Nicole, you need to acquire some money and invest it into a piece of property."

What would make him think that I could afford to buy property? I posed that question to him and he responded with something I'll never forget: "What makes you think you can't?"

I have noticed that intelligent people always have quick responses. They tend to answer a question with a question in a way that forces you to think. I rattled off several reasons that came to mind, "I'm broke. I don't have any money right now. I'm trying to get myself out of debt."

Cleveland said, "Okay. You've told me about some of the barriers. Fair enough. Now tell me how you're going to get *beyond* the barriers, because you can't let them stop you from reaching success or obtaining a goal."

I pondered those words for a moment before saying, "Teach me! Teach me what I need to know, and if I think this is something I can do, I'll do it."

Wow! I remember like it was yesterday—being so inspired by those simple, thought-provoking words that came from his mouth and the more powerful ones that followed. So, soon thereafter, I bought a building, and began to live rent free. Cleveland showed me on paper how it was done. He broke down the costs of a mortgage on a two flat, rent that I could collect and other ways to make money from the building. He showed me that instead of paying so much in taxes, I could actually recuperate more funds each year. Right away, he made me understand everything about the numbers in real estate that would help make changes in my finances.

Everything he said made sense to me, but deep down inside I wasn't sure if I could do it. The more I listened to him the more the desire to actually become a real estate professional grew. First, I prayed about it, then I increased my investment again—the maximum this time—which I believe was twelve percent. Where I had started off with zero, one short year later, I had now acquired almost six thousand in stock funding and was eligible for a withdrawal as a first-time home buyer. I was a little scared, but Cleveland told me that when I bought a building, I would make money every single month. He said that even when I closed on the building, I was going to walk away with a check.

I started dating another young man at the time. The day he walked into the building with me, he had an extremely negative response. He tried to discourage me in every way possible. Boyfriend #2 visited the place before I purchased it and said, "What a foolish thing you're doing. Saving all of your money . . . can't even get your hair done. All for a building. How stupid is that?" Now mind you, he worked at a health center which seemed to be all he aspired to do in life at the time. Limited thinking!

In February 1994, I made a down payment with funds I had saved and purchased my first building in my early twenties. Cleveland was right. I actually came back with a check for nearly $3,000 after closing. I was amazed! I moved in the first floor, had a husband and wife as tenants upstairs, and intended to rent the basement apartment to a college student.

My dad, "Mr. Entroproknow" himself, shared encouraging words with me. "Nicko" (his nickname for me), "When are you going to get building number two? I'm proud of you, girl."

Those two sentences pumped life back into my mission. It was a wonderful feeling that someone from my immediate family felt I was truly making great decisions. When was I going to get building number two? Indeed!

Now the dynamics of my life had changed. I paid off most of my debt, was collecting a rent check, and was making a profit. The easy yet foolish choice would be to do my favorite thing—go on a spending spree. But instead, I had been bitten by the real estate bug. The first thought that came to mind was——how about reinvesting to buy another building? And that's exactly what I did.

As I continued to make investment after investment,

my business grew substantially, and I was becoming the entrepreneur my dad said I could be. I was exceeding, not just meeting, all expectations I held for my professional life. Before I could blink twice, I had 15 properties and was now the second vice president over corporate division services at TNT.

During what should have been the happiest time of my life, I had one major problem——the wrong man by my side. Everything in my life was going well except for pains I experienced from being involved with a man who didn't honor me or himself. The more successful I became, the more hateful he turned.

Though I heard about it in books, saw it in movies and on television, this would be the first time I personally experienced domestic violence in any form. It seems I couldn't do anything right. Everything was my fault. He resented my desire for more, and it became the strongest sentiment in that relationship for seven *long* years. I endured verbal, mental and, on occasion, physical abuse—all for the sake of what I thought was love once again. Inwardly, I knew differently. Even with everything I had going for me, I couldn't see a way out. My self-esteem hit an all-time low, and the courage and qualities I valued in my business life—taking risks, investing, helping employees, encouraging others—were simply non-existent when it came to this man.

My employees rose above being Client Service Associates and Representatives to receiving titles like Officer, Second Vice President, Manager, and more, simply because I showed them I believed in them. This was my survival technique as I walked through life, traveled through dark times alone, holding my head up, and keeping up appearances. Where was my light? Where was that inner strength that could help me say, "To hell with him. I deserve better. God didn't make me or mold me to become someone else's punching bag or someone else's place to dump all his anger and frustrations."

The women who worked under me excelled and made it into positions beyond their own dreams. Their successes became my light.

One morning I woke up, looked to my right and said, "What the hell is wrong with me? Why am I remaining side by side with someone who has no respect for women, let alone me?" My whole life was dedicated to helping women get to the next level. I worked in a shelter seeing abused women daily, volunteered my time to encourage them, and sympathized with them. The troubling part of my great work was that I didn't even recognize myself, "Ms. Has it All Together," as one of them.

Somehow, the illusion of my success was a better shield than any other. My businesses were going very well, and no one could see through the role I portrayed which enabled me to keep deeply hidden secrets of pain, hurt, degradation and mistreatment. Sometimes, one simple thing could lift my spirits. When I bought a new pair of shoes——a tall pair of gorgeous heels, sharp stilettos, or some funky mules——and put them on my feet I felt empowered, even if it was only temporary. My thoughts were that when the world looks up to you, you have to put in an appearance: you must "show up" even when you know you're living a lie.

Now herein lies the lesson. Remember I had an issue with the young lady at the gym? She would teach one thing, but her habits, appearance and actions were the direct opposite? Life helped drive the point home. I was teaching women everything from self-esteem building to self-motivation techniques, but I needed the class myself. I knew what to do; I just didn't do it. Those who can't do, teach. Right? My thinking held me as a willing prisoner: I can't be that woman that travels from man to man. I'd soon become some worn out pair of shoes. So instead, I stayed and became just like that pair of shoes we tend to wear down to the ground then toss in the back of the closet. Females have a tendency to stay with men that are not good for them, just to make a point that is practically irrelevant. A man cannot love you when he doesn't love himself, and it is a useless mission to search for a microscopic tidbit of love inside of him. This is not your job, it is up to the Creator. Spend your time more wisely, "praying for guidance" and then "building a spiritual and well-organized plan for your life."

The day I decided to do just what the Snoop Dogg song states and "drop him like he was hot," was the day I became empowered again. Right then and there, I vowed never to make that mistake again. Although I lived it, knew better, and wanted better for myself, learning lessons on a personal level was a lot harder than getting out of that college debt. My lack of self-confidence drove me into making decisions that did not honor me. To change the pattern, I began to reflect daily upon the amazing gifts given to me and spotlight my talents, beauty (both inner and outer), appearance while meditating on the future I desired. What worked for me will work for you too.

Yes, I believe in the old saying that, "If you look good, you feel good." We should all wake up every morning and strive to look our absolute best, and that in some ways boosts our spirits. However, we must remember that while we are transforming the outer appearance – we're also working internally to build self-confidence and self-esteem to change our attitude. Begin to think positive thoughts and say only positive words about yourself and others. You will begin to see a new reflection in the mirror...a Cinderella or Prince Charming special effect will occur...your glass slipper

Chapter 3: Ponder over these questions

Nothing in life is easy...however, it is possible: what sacrifices will you make to achieve your mission in life? Build your self-confidence by affirming daily, "I am beautiful from the inside out...I'm open to receive all that the world has for me and more."

Who do you need to remove from your life that is, simply put, "a dream thief?"

Write your thoughts in your journal.

"Too often we underestimate the power of a touch, a smile, a kind word, a listening ear, an honest accomplishment, or the smallest act of caring, all of which have the potential to turn a life around."
- Leo Buscaglia

CHAPTER 4

LIFE WAITS FOR NO ONE...STEP ON REGARDLESS OF
WHAT LIES AHEAD

We've discussed how important it is to embrace every essence of life because it waits for no one. Neither me...nor you.

Build up your self-esteem. Take full accountability for the new life that is waiting for you. Over the past 10 years, I've met so many young women and men suffering from weight issues: some for being underweight and not feeling "filled out" or buff enough, and others suffering from over eating and pressure to get rid of excess weight.

Obesity rates in the United States have risen to an all time high. In 2004, there was a research report written about a study that lasted from 1999 to 2002 entitled "Prevalence of overweight and obesity among children and adolescents: United States" conducted by the CDC. According to that report, "16 % children (over 9 million) 6-19 year olds are overweight or obese" which is three times what it was in 1980. In addition, this report brings out the fact that also during this same time period an additional 15% were "at risk of becoming overweight". Not only has this number tripled, but in the past three decades (according to this same study) obesity has "more than doubled" in both children and adolescents from ages 2-5 and also ages 12-19 while more than tripling in children between the ages of 6-11. Many children, teenagers and young adults face severe health challenges and even premature death due to their poor food choices. We can visually see how eating these foods can affect the body and overall physical condition of a person. What the visible eye can't see is the internal pain, the inner shame and self-hatred overweight or underweight young people face because they are unwilling to love themselves for who or what they are.

During a conversation I once had with a young woman she told me, "I am tired of being called fat, and it hurts me that I can't lose all the weight that I've gained. I don't feel attractive. I envy other women with great shapes, because I wish that I had their figure. I'm not happy with who I am and I don't think it will ever change."

My response to her was very simple. "Sweetheart, if you place a limit on your abilities...limitations will be exactly your end result. If you transform your mind about your situation and center the attention on the problem area, there will be much required for you to accomplish this goal...but it is possible. Let's get over thinking that this will be an easy mission. It isn't, but with hard work and discipline you can lose weight and feel great internally and externally."

As of today, you can no longer say what is "mission impossible" in your life. Begin to vision a "New You".

Create a vision board for yourself. Put motivating and inspiring words on it. Wake up every day saying, "Today is a new day that brings about new opportunities". Say it out loud, "I am special and powerful. I have the power to change every area of my life; there is nothing that I can't accomplish." You must tackle your weight issues the same way you have to study and practice to increase your grades. Practice, be determined to succeed and eat differently. If you begin to remove chips, soda pop and fried foods from your life and replace them with sautéed spinach, broccoli, baked chicken, yogurt and other healthy items, you will become a healthier individual. In addition, dedicate time to exercise. You know exactly what to do. Get serious about it and do it. You are the only person holding you back. Millions of people have put forth the time, dedication and effort to change their weight and self-confidence. If you have decided to accept the shape and form you currently are, then begin to love who you have designed yourself to be and find peace with it. But please do not stay in this position because you fear failing and not achieving your goal. Affirm, "I am powerful beyond my imagination and can change anything." Now I want to share with you the story of my sister, Jeanette Johnson.

Sudden changes can occur, be prepared for all things...Increase your Faith

A couple of months prior to making the final decision to leave Boyfriend #2, one of the most tragic situations in my life to date occurred. This situation put many things into perspective for me. I remember the day so very clearly—when once again, I was upset about my decision to even be in this relationship with a man who did not honor me.

After a long strenuous day at TNT and completing a few hours of community service, I headed home. I was only blocks away from my house when I felt a sudden urge to go to my parents' home. For some reason, I just wanted to take some time and speak to my dad who, by now, was my best friend and a man I began to hug as often as I could. So, I quickly made a right turn off South Shore Drive and headed to my parents' house. It seemed like he was sitting there on the porch waiting just for me, when in actuality this was just his "spot" since he retired and had nothing on his agenda but fishing. I knew he loved my visits, and I loved being there with him just as much. I was so proud of him because once he retired from work, he went back to school and started from 3rd grade until he graduated from 8th grade. He went to an adult learning facility and said, "I will not be denied an education." You should not deny yourself of an education either.

Not even ten minutes after I arrived, a Ford Explorer pulled up. The face on the driver's side seemed unfamiliar, but the woman on the passenger side was none other than my lovely sister, Netty. I couldn't believe how beautiful she looked on this day. Let me just share a brief story with you. Netty suffered from severe self-esteem issues. Even with the most beautiful face and voice like a hummingbird, she had a weakness; we all have one or even a few. Mine were men and shoes. Netty's was food.

For ten years, Netty lived in the Chicago Housing Authority, more commonly known as "the projects." One day my mom and I went to pick her up. My mom cried so hard because of what we saw—the apartment was in total disarray in nearly deplorable conditions. Netty stayed in my mother's home for ten years after that day. We sat in the kitchen once, and she described how she wanted to get a job and have her own place. Something inside of her feared change so much that she didn't believe in herself at all.

Typically when I saw her, Netty was dressed in clothing better suited for a woman who didn't come from a caring family. However, on this day that I sat on the porch with my father, she was glowing in a beautiful peach dress with her hair pulled up and make-up beautifully done. A few weeks earlier she began to practice uplifting, self-motivation techniques, ones we would rehearse in the kitchen together. The many positive things I saw in her, she was finally beginning to see in herself. She spoke life back into her body, her mind and her soul.

Netty had been living on her own now for three months. She had a job as an inventory clerk at a grocery store. It was a start, a place to move up from where she had become comfortable, and that was a huge step. She didn't move far from my parents, because she still needed support. She courageously made a decision to change her life after 20 years of suffering and was now experiencing happiness beyond her imagination.

Oh, what a pleasure it was to see her walking up to the porch that day. I kept complimenting her, "Oh, Netty, you look so beautiful."

She kept saying, "Huh?"

So I repeated it again.

And at her constant reply of, "Huh?"

I ended up saying it over seven times. And finally she replied with a simple, "Thank you." I slipped her some pocket change and minutes later I proudly watched her ride away.

The next morning I was on the clock at TNT. My supervisor rushed in the room, interrupting a meeting I was a part of and said, "I need to speak with you right away."

I was a complete workaholic and was offended by interruptions during times of business, but the look on my supervisor's face concerned me much more than it offended me.

We stepped into the hallway and she said, "Your mother and father need you to call them at home."

Naturally, my heart was pounding as I continued to probe and ask questions, but she kept simply saying, "You should call home."

I called the house and my dad answered, saying, "Nicky, Netty's in the hospital. You should come on home and we can go there together."

I was thinking, "Dad, what's wrong? Is it her varicose veins?" She's used to going back and forth to the hospital dealing with the painful effects of varicose veins. No big deal. Nevertheless, my Dad told me to hurry home. I left work right then and there. People kept asking to drive me home, but I refused their offers. Thinking that nothing could be seriously wrong, I got in my convertible, dropped the top and turned on the radio before a sudden urge made me call home again.

This time my dad's voice was not so calm. In fact, he seemed a little hysterical, which was completely out of character for him. By this time I pleaded with my dad to tell me what was wrong. "Netty is gone. Netty is gone." My father had only cried once that I could remember when his older brother died. Hearing his sorrow over the phone brought an instant sickness inside of me.

I made a U-turn and after that I really can't tell you all that happened next. I can only remember someone from my job driving me to my parent's home. I was in the back seat feeling as though everything, every movement was part of a dream—someone else's dream. It did not feel real to me. I kept thinking this must be a mistake and when I arrive everything will be just fine. I can't even remember which co-worker drove me home that day. When we pulled up on the block, my dad helped me from the car, holding me tight as both of us cried tears of sorrow. The tears in his face hurt me beyond any words. I was still in disbelief even though my dad would never lie about something so serious. The reality of my sister's death was just too much for me. I could not accept the report that I was given. All I could manage to ask was, "Where is she? Where is she?"

My co-worker graciously drove both of us to Little Company of Mary Hospital. My mom and the rest of the family were already there. I walked into the morgue, and against my mother's wishes wanted to see Netty. How could I believe she was gone unless I saw it with my own eyes? I had just witnessed her transformation the day before. She was overweight and had been for many years, but yesterday she looked better than ever...the happiest I'd ever seen her since we were kids. She was a beacon of light that shined so very brightly. How? Oh God...How could this happen to her? Why now? I have so many questions, and I need answers to this madness NOW.

Every step I took into the morgue felt like my feet were weighed down as the long hallway seemed to grow before me. Minutes seemed like forever before I walked into the room and over to the cold, steel table where her body lay. I understood immediately why my mother didn't want me to see her. Netty suffered a massive heart attack and rigor mortis stiffened her body. Her hands and arms were frozen in a position behind her head. Her face was twisted in pain, and it was a sight that left me filled with fear, misery and nightmares for several weeks after her death.

At that moment I was so angry with God. Why

would He do this to her? How could He let this happen to her?" She spent most of her life being depressed, feeling down and never following her dreams. Finally, when she decided to take a stand in her life to change it for the better, in return she faced death. What sense did that make? The thought itself brought an overwhelming sense of grief and unfairness.

Months afterward, as my anger dissipated, the fear went away and the nightmares subsided. Clearly, the Creator made sure I learned a lesson by speaking once again in that still voice saying, "Don't take life for granted. Your life belongs to me." And from Netty's transition, I simply understood that life could end at any time.

This motivated me to walk away from that painful relationship with Boyfriend #2. I later learned that Boyfriend #2 was just another young man traveling through life without a road map. I don't believe that his true intentions were to incite pain in my life. I simply believe in the old saying, "hurt people...hurt people." However, it is important to state that anyone who is not honoring you is completely unacceptable. This is non-negotiable.

The experience with Netty also encouraged me to begin to truly live. Even though I made money, I didn't do much else for myself. I was still skeptical about spending money (except on shoes), because I knew what it was like not to have any.

I started taking vacations, having pamper days and even implemented a yearly "birthday celebration" for each member of my immediate family. I embraced life and cherished it. And although I missed my dear Netty, I learned something valuable from her death as I did from her life. When she decided to change, she did—and did it wholeheartedly. We could all see the effects that her inner change made on her outer appearance.

More than anything I will continue to hold that image of her walking up the porch draped in that peach dress, with her dark brown eyes alive with power and confidence. For every tragic situation that has ever occurred in my life... a great victory soon followed. Let me explain to you exactly what I mean. Life experiences happen to help us become stronger and better. If we were not afflicted with any type of opposition that tested our faith, how would we grow? My sister's death was, initially, very difficult for me to handle. As time passed, I was rejuvenated with ideas and thoughts on how to ensure other young teenagers would learn how to move beyond the internal pain caused by low self-esteem.

My life had a new design...it was meant to help teenagers and young adults around the world to believe in themselves. This message educates others on how they must be their own human iPod and learn how to confidently and boldly speak positive words back into their lives to ensure success. An iPod is used to play your favorite songs. Often we put on R. Kelly, Kanye West, Alicia Keys or some other artist to encourage ourselves. We must do the same mentally with the iPod in our thoughts and turn up the words that will inspire us when we are down and build us up when we feel broken. At times, I must amplify my iPod and tell myself, "You are beautiful...inside and out. There is nothing you can't accomplish if you simply believe."

Today, you must become your own self-motivator. You must empower yourself and stop waiting for someone else to give you information that is uplifting. The moment a pity party even looks like it is about to come, turn up your iPod, which is your secret weapon, in your head and speak positive affirmations over your life. "You CAN get an A at out of that class. You WILL make the track team if you try. You CAN keep out of trouble regardless of your friends, because you're not a follower." Find the words that you must speak over your life to take it up another level to ensure victory. One of the most powerful statements I ever heard was when listening to *The Magic Story*. It stated, "FAILURE ONLY EXIST IN THE GRAVE." If you are still living, you have a new opportunity to build every area of your self-being to make improvements.

Chapter 4:Ponder over these questions

Taking Your Self-Esteem and Self-Image to the Next Level

Get in front of that mirror on a daily basis and begin to see your true beauty that is instilled both internally and externally. SPEAK into the mirror and declare, "I am amazing and successful. I am SUCCESS...S.U.C.C.E.S.S. There is nothing that I can't conquer with FAITH. I BELIEVE in myself. Victory belongs to me." Find the words that you need, and use them as often as needed. The only way to combat negative self-talk is with positive statements. Give yourself a new opportunity at an improved life by practicing your self-esteem enhancement technique daily. Sit back and watch how you begin to grow exponentially.

Write out your feelings about these thoughts in your journal.

"Nature often holds up a mirror so we can see more clearly the ongoing processes of growth, renewal, and transformation in our lives." - Mary Ann Brussant

I am not afraid...I was born to do this. - Joan of Arc

CHAPTER 5

FIGHTING TO MAKE YOUR WAY THROUGH ADVERSITY

If you limit yourself before you start you won't finish the race. My god-daughter wanted to run track but she constantly spoke words like, "I'm not good enough, I can't do it, and others are better than me." So, naturally when she entered into races her performances were not successful, and she didn't win any races just as she said she wouldn't. There's power in words. You can speak negativity or positivity into existence. One day, after taking time to understand the dynamic laws of prosperity, my god-daughter began to scream the words, " I AM SUCCESS. S.U.C.C.E.S.S."

During her next track meet, instead of speaking words of lack and limitation she declared, " I AM SUCCESS. S.U.C.C.E.S.S." over and over again. She screamed it as she ran without being conscientiously aware of her placement in the race….she ran and screamed while affirming good things into existence. YES! YES! She won the race. She acquired a winning mentality and continued to win races, because the power she possessed to accomplish the task existed deep inside of her. She just had to begin to speak and affirm it. When she changed her thoughts from negative, limited ones, she graduated to greater success because she spoke it over her life. There is power in this statement. You can speak it right before cheerleading try-outs, before you hit the stage to audition for your dream role, and even before walking in class to take that last, big test. These powerful, amazing words can affirm greatness back into your life. Naturally, you must study more and practice just like many great athletes such as Michael Jordan or phenomenal dancers such as the Alvin Ailey dancers. These people are no different than you.

Regardless of all the odds stacked against me, by maintaining my success mentality, I was able to "win, win, win no matter WHAT!"

You can do anything that you put your mind to...just believe.

Like putting on a new pair of shoes, dropping the dead weight of fear and anxiety over things that I could not change made me feel revived and ready to conquer the world. My career was still on the rise, and now I could focus on another part of my dream. I was drawn back to the time when I was a child when everything revolved around the community and our church. I truly understood that giving back and community work was just as important as excelling in my career. So, just as I made it a habit to tithe ten percent of my income, I began to dedicate thirty percent of my time every week to helping others. I already started spending time in shelters helping women build their self-esteem while I was working to build my own. I had accumulated many properties, was promoted to second vice president at TNT, and was now making a major difference in the communities I was born and raised in and many others just like them.

Although I spent many years working in corporate America, I had another dream burning inside of me. This one would force me to drop everything and begin to pursue my true calling and passion. I didn't have a clue of exactly what I wanted to do, but I knew I had accumulated wealth and needed to invest quickly. By now, I had excellent credit, and stepping out on faith to do something courageous was another brick in the foundation. Several community events I attended with residents, politicians and other business owners were filled with constant complaints that steady, viable and sustainable businesses didn't exist in our communities. After a short time passed, my thoughts ran to being part of the solution instead of complaining about the problem.

Yes, it's a cliché, but it fit the situation. I once attended a community affair and a Chicago politician stood up confidently and said, "I hear your complaints about what we don't have and understand it, but we must focus on determining how we can build a better quality of life for all." And then he delivered a powerful blow by saying, "With all of your love and desire to build a community, why not consider building a business? The same type of business that you're requesting "outside" people to come in to build, build it yourself!"

Sleep didn't come easy that night. His words kept going through my mind over and over again. What kind of business could I build to help supply a need in my neighborhood? I vowed to pray daily for direction until I received an answer.

Things were going so well. I had a house built from the ground up, rental property, two cars. I had everything on the surface that the average American person wants—everything except love.

What exactly is love? R Kelly has a new song and explains when a young woman loves, she loves for real. This is true. When a young man loves, he can love for real also. Looking back, I don't think I knew exactly what it was. Love means different things to different people. Young women especially define love in terms of "I love you unconditionally," or it may be, "I love you as long as you do a, b and c." Often young men put it in terms that are drastically different— "I love you, in my own way." This may not translate into that unconditional, all-consuming, self-sacrificing kind of love that is expected on a deeper level. Few people can attain this kind of love, because they, like me, have not learned one valuable lesson: love yourself first and then love others. Those who have not learned this important lesson are destined to repeat past mistakes. Loving yourself is not a difficult task. You must begin to do small things daily to encourage yourself, affirm goodness back into your life with positive words, and on occasion treat yourself to some of life's many great pleasures.

Please listen clearly. The word LOVE sounds so simple, but is often quite complicated. Picture a person in your life that you LOVE right now whether it is your parents, friends, family members or care giver. Do you have the image of that person in your mind right now? Hold it for a few minutes...It feels good to think about that person doesn't it? Now think about someone that you claim to "can't stand," or even claim to hate. Can you picture that person? Ok...hold on to the image of them in your mind for a minute. Now here comes the tough part; you must learn to love them, too. WHAT? Yes, you must learn to love your enemies. If not, the hurt, pain and weight of whatever made you begin to dislike them will block your blessings to a fruitful life. The NIV version of the Bible quotes this Scripture, "Love endures long and is patient and kind; love never is envious nor boils over with jealousy, it is not boastful or vainglorious, does not display itself haughtily." God commands us to love our enemies in Luke 6:27-29, "But I tell you who hear me: Love your enemies, do well to those who hate you, bless those who curse you, pray for those who mistreat you."

I know you are thinking, "No way...I can't do it". I'm here to tell you, "YES YOU CAN!" and you MUST...if not for them, you must do it for yourself. Grab a hold of the picture of the person that you dislike again...HOLD it. Now remind yourself that God loves this person as much as He loves you. We are all made in the image and likeness of God. It doesn't matter that we made mistakes, we will probably make mistakes until we leave this earth...you have made mistakes with other people as well.

You are wasting your energy hating another human being made in the same image that you are. They are a child of God just like you regardless of their crime. You must invoke the power of love upon people today. When you allow your heart to heal, you open up a flow of prosperity into your life. Soon the wounds heal and you realize that this person is human just like you and that we all make mistakes. I know you're wondering, "How can I begin to love someone that I dislike". You must vision them daily with love. You must ask for healing and speak words of affirmation of love upon this person. To remain bitter, angry, and disgruntled only robs one person from a fantastic life... YOU.

Holding on to pain and lacking the ability to forgive will strip you of lifelong happiness. It isn't attractive to hold grudges or stand firm in unforgiveness. We have all hurt and fallen short of the expectation of another person at some point in life. How easily we forget our on mistakes, but refuse to forgive others for theirs. Yes, I am telling you that no matter what, you must forgive. You must forgive the person that may have robbed you, molested you, stole your soul mate, murdered a family member or friend, lied on you, talked about you and mistreated you. Yes, you must forgive them all. To live in a constant state of hatred, anger or frustration is accepting defeat. In being unforgiving, you allow them to win, steal your joy and capture your emotions. This leads to trust issues and emotional roadblocks, even for those who meant us no harm, for fear of being hurt again. Forgive!

From my experiences, I learned to take full responsibility for my choices. My relationship with God was restored, and I did everything it took to ensure that connection was solid and unshakeable. I then began to study and learn the dynamic laws of prosperity in my life and discovered that if I changed my thoughts everything around me could become better. The fact was real simple; I could change every single thing about me, but I most certainly could not change another person. Believing you have the power to change someone else will always lead to failure. Focus on yourself and being the best YOU you can be. Build up your mind. Think prosperous thoughts. Remove thoughts of failure, or lack or limitation. You have the internal power to develop new skills. You must become your #1 fan.

During my transition I had to re-evaluated myself. Why did I constantly choose people who were not right for me? What was I missing? My assessment period forced me to search the root cause of my actions, which took me back to the Mary Jane days. I had to admit that even though the imagery on the outside looked like I was at the top of my game, I was still suffering from low self-esteem . . . just like my sister Netty, but in a different form. At times, you can find yourself judging everyone and everything about other people. It is so easy to analyze everyone else's area of weakness. This is a self-esteem issue that justifies tearing down another person's greatness. Have you ever found yourself looking at another young woman or man and thinking, "Who do they think they are?" All he/she/they did was walk into the room with a look of confidence. Why are you analyzing this person? What is making you take time from your schedule to give this amount of attention to someone you do not even know? Did this individual's level of confidence intimidate you?

During my self-assessment period, instead of "Pointing the finger" at anyone else, I pointed my finger directly at myself—my choices, my actions, my life. There was no one else to blame. I had a God complex, assuming that I—an attractive, hard-working, determined woman who would look good on any man's arm——had the power to change someone other than myself. I had the magic wand with the ability of making a man from mediocre to king of the castle. Wrong! Now I had to go to the back of my closet, pull out those combat boots, slip them on, tie them up and get to stepping. The real work was just beginning.

There is a major difference between the love you receive from God and the love you receive from human beings. God's love is eternal, yet our love is temporary. People love you until something goes wrong. Then they disregard you or have an overwhelming, consuming hatred for you. True love sees beyond your faults. True love forgives. True love understands that people make mistakes. True love for yourself allows you to forgive others as you desire to be forgiven.

One of the most difficult things in life is to review your own faults. It takes courage to stand before that mirror and say, "Stop blaming everybody. You are part of this problem." After doing this, I had to tackle my desperate need for love. It's not a bad thing to want love, but it is unhealthy to feel as if you need it from another human being instead of first accepting the love from God, the source of our supply, and then loving yourself next. This is the basis for a boundless number of issues in my life. I made a personal, emotional and spiritual "to do" list which encompassed two major things: time for me to learn to love myself and how to depend on the Lord instead of a man. I will be the first to admit that this journey was (and still is) difficult, but it is possible. I take it day by day and remind myself that I can truly do all things.

Another breakthrough came by removing every negative entity in my life. Instead of judging others,

I analyzed myself; in actuality, I spent the majority of the time making self-improvements. It was time to be a little selfish, and for the record, that's okay. People often give so much of their lives to others they don't take time for themselves. The truth of the matter is that when our relationships with friends, family and others fall apart, everything else follows suit. Sometimes sticking with a plan of self first and others second means we gain our center and have something to share with others.

The moment my daily ritual of prayer became second nature, it led me to the realization that I had even more dreams which hadn't been realized. At this point, I decided to go back to the dream of building a business within the community. One cold winter morning in my beautiful greystone building, I woke up around three o'clock screaming in my sleep, because I finally knew what I wanted to do. Since my childhood, I would gaze into the windows of shoe stores and stand in awe of their beauty, always fantasizing about their beautiful shoes being on my feet. Every time I felt down or lacked the love I wanted from men in my life, buying a new pair of shoes always made me feel temporarily empowered. Shoes had a way of making me happy, and I knew that other women shared this same passion.

When I rose later that morning, the message from God was very clear. Now it was up to me. I could allow this dream to die right away, which is typical of people with great ideas, or I could choose to give it life. Now the truth of the matter was that I had never worked in a retail store environment, but that little fact wasn't going stop me. One thing had always been clear to me; if you don't know something, you always have an opportunity to learn it. So, it was time to get on the learning train again, which was not new to me. After all, I hadn't been on the express train in the banking industry, the local to stocks and investing, and finished up with a commuter ride into the real estate world. All aboard!

The very next morning, I made thirty signs which read:

I want to buy your building, please call me. Followed by my number.

I drove down Cottage Grove Avenue, which was filled with distressed properties—a far cry from a place where one would open a store that was supposed to rival the kind on Rodeo Drive. The community, called Bronzeville, was once filled with successful businesses. During the recession in the 1950s, a lot of those businesses closed and created a void that no one knew how to fill. Black people were living in the high point of prime property just a few blocks from the lakefront, minutes from downtown and with connections to every major expressway in Chicago. One would say my choice to build a business in this area is the first major mistake in retail; typically location is key to the success of a retail business. On the other *foot*, this vision to build the property somewhere in this area was a burning desire in my heart. My logic for even entertaining the thought of having a business in the community was simple: the city was beginning to reinvest in the area, pumping millions of dollars into redevelopment with the intent to usher in another group of people and culture vastly different from the brown-skinned, enterprising people who had been there for decades.

Driving past the places many investors had overlooked, the risk-taker in me stood at army attention. I already knew it would be hard work to market and promote the type of business I had in mind, but I never resist a challenge. If I put my time, money and energy into this business idea, it could——and would—— prosper. No matter the area, no matter that people thought my idea of a shoe salon flanked by a car-filled lot on one side and a vacant lot on the other within the heart of Bronzeville was totally insane. Yet, I remained optimistic.

As I traveled that morning placing signs on every building I came across, there was one in particular that stood out the most. The windows were covered so I couldn't see inside, but measuring it from the outside, it was a lot of space. In my mind's eye I envisioned building a business rivaling those on the Magnificent Mile, one that could hold enough women to host community events right in my place of business instead of running from shelter to shelter.

I left a note and walked quietly to my car, praying all the way, knowing I wouldn't visit any more properties or leave any other notes that day. Now there was much more work to do: getting incorporated, devising a business plan, securing financing, building a website, and the biggest hurdle yet, getting the community to support this idea. Actually the community would buy into any possible retail idea to help get the economy moving and the alderman was a vision-forward woman who did everything by the rules. I met with her first to discuss my plans.

I could never understand businesses that would build in communities and never give back. I saw it from every place that I lived but especially in the African-American community.   Other cultures would come in, conduct business, and never attend a community meeting or have a day to give back to the people who patronize their business regularly. Some business owners treated the people who placed money in their pocket without any respect, simply because their options seemed limited. Those are pimps —just without the suit, big, feather-brimmed hat and the "tricked-out" Cadillac. I couldn't run a business in any community and not contribute to it. Even now, I believe community residents should hold business owners accountable for giving back to the community surrounding the business.

Residents in some deprived neighborhoods constantly settle for less. Recently, I went to a local gas station which is located in a predominately African-American area and witnessed the most repulsive client service I could ever imagine. The cashier, possibly the owner, had received his money from a young gentleman, but was more concerned with collecting the money from other customers waiting in the line than finishing the young man's transaction.

Without any hesitation the young gentleman asked nicely, "Can you please turn my pump on sir?"

To my surprise the clerk screamed back, "Wait a minute!" Then he said out loud, "He's acting like a damn animal!"

I couldn't believe my ears. How could he disrespect this man who had just supported his business? I stepped in immediately and said to him in a voice loud enough for everyone to hear, "You have the nerve to disrespect him? Your words were unkind and completely unnecessary." I told him that I was disappointed in his behavior and chose to take my money somewhere else. Everyone else in line heard what he had said to this young man, yet everyone remained in line. Please note that in this neighborhood, many residents have complained continuously about being mistreated at this gas station, yet they still support it. Why?

Early on I set a goal. I wouldn't let a single day go by without doing something related to my new business plan, even if I just made a phone call. I set up a meeting with my Alderman, Toni Preckwinkle, and community liaisons to discuss my plans. They loved the idea and supported it wholeheartedly. Within one week, mostly all of the legal aspects of starting the business were done. All was going well. The second week, reality set in. I didn't know *anything* about running a retail store. I needed direction on the first steps. How do I buy? Where do I get my products? How much do I buy? Where do I get a register from? How do I pay sales taxes? I didn't have a clue but knew who did!

I had developed a list for my personal development, spiritual development and real estate endeavors, so I needed to put one together for this retail business. I reviewed websites and conducted library research to make a list of other successful shoe businesses. Next, I called them up, one by one, to ask their expert opinion on how I could successfully open a retail store. Seventy percent of the people I called wouldn't speak to me. I couldn't believe how many people felt intimidated by a potentially new business in the same field. My major issue in life was how I felt about myself and about my choices in men. On a business level, I always wanted to share with others and see people achieve success. I couldn't understand why these businesses were closing their doors on me and refusing to provide professional advice.

The journey into the retail side of business was tougher than I ever imagined. I can't tell you how many people shut the door in my face or said things to discourage me. I knew that I would need to press on, and thanks to the thirty percent that would talk to me, I would make it.

One wonderful woman, who owned *Gabrielle's* on the north side of Chicago, opened up her heart, her mind and her store for me to learn. I also had someone else to invite me into another store but later learned it was for all the wrong reasons. This individual only wanted to know my plans to block my path. How tragic! This time when the caution sign blinked into view, I listened and kept my focus on the people who would help. Being treated so poorly by other entrepreneurs who had the same passions stopped hurting after a while. One major thing helped me in that process; I accepted that those people didn't understand that God knew their address and would not mix their blessings with anyone else's. All I could do was pray for them, and I made a vow to never become one of them. Then...I kept it moving forward.

Each day as I began to understand my destiny more and more, the fear dwindled and my focus stayed on the mission. Building a business on a desolate street would not be an easy task. I was tired of hearing complaints about what our community lacked. I would be a pioneer, the brave one, and provide what was needed. I loved everything about shoes . . . loved the way they felt when being slipped on my feet and also the versatility shoes added to my wardrobe.

Any woman can tell you it is an empowering experience when you find the right pair of shoes. Even with guys when they put on a clean pair of sparkling white new gym shoes...wow. However, I could not just open any kind of shoe store ... no way ... no how. I had to open one that defined the very essence of a woman. I started with the store's color. I wanted to take women back to their childhood days and dazzle them in pinkness. Pink is a simple but bold color that can be sassy, sultry and symbolic of a woman's touch. Then the interior of the store had to be comfortable, relaxing and inviting. I wanted women to feel like queens when they walked in the door; experience royalty in gracing my business with their glorious presence; and find value in spending money in my store which, in turn, would keep the doors open indefinitely.

The chairs I selected were massive, relaxed and antique in style. I ordered glass tables to showcase the products, which sat upon beautiful pink stands and pink hat boxes. Detail and attention were put into the café station, so when people entered into the shoe salon they felt personalized attention. Since I was a bargain shopper myself, I knew that just because I didn't spend thousands at a time on purchases didn't mean my customers should not feel as though they entered an expensive, elaborate shopping paradise every time they entered my store.

Most businesses have strayed away from providing superior customer service because the Internet has become the way to handle exchanges. Sales are conducted without ever seeing a face, hearing a voice or connecting with an individual. In contrast, I love interacting with a woman who is on the prowl for a great pair of shoes. She walks in under the impression that she really knows what she is seeking. She is on a "shoe high," the same kind of high she would get when walking into a special event with a sharp dress, hair laid, make-up on point, while watching the eye of every man to ensure all eyes are on "The Queen." This is how a serious shoe shopper views a trip to her favorite shoe store. Yes, I say this with ease and experience ... a simple pair of shoes can instantly change the way a woman feels.

For any information other entrepreneurs tried to hide from me, God somehow saw to it that I received everything I needed to start ... and more. I signed up to attend a merchandiser shoe show and arrived on the first day ready to shop.

Understand this point clearly: if you are focused on your dream and something is for you, no one can keep it away from you. No one! I can't say enough that God knows your address; information is in abundance to Him. Someone, somewhere taught you what you are doing.

Why would you selfishly deny success to someone else?

Something inside of me was changing. I would be remiss if I didn't mention that I have wonderful, God-fearing girlfriends. There are two in particular, Janine and Tiffany, who held the vision strong even when others couldn't manage a single encouraging word. My "soul" sisters prayed with me, fasted on my behalf and believed in the miracle of my future.

My good friends Tenyka and Jessica also served as guardian angels on earth to help me build my dreams, and Carla, Debbie and San called me and asked, "Nick, what can I do to help girl?"

Rhea and Michelle, my two childhood friends from my parent's block had my back. They stayed in my presence and supported me all along the way. My friends marveled at my vision of opening the store and supported me to the ends of earth. I love them dearly for their commitment. Rhea even moved forward with her dream business and opened RH Dance and Performing Arts school. Her school is one of the most amazing and entertaining dance/modeling schools that I've ever laid eyes upon. She takes a student and teaches them how to bring out every gift that is hidden inside of them…it's amazing.

There were some people close to me, however, who became extremely jealous and envious in ways that I had not previously experienced; that took me by surprise. When you are working to build your dreams, some people take it personally and because they lack a sense of direction, motivation and encouragement to do the same, they find fault in everything you do. It comes out in the smallest things, like little verbal hints, "Yeah, she has new friends around all of a sudden. Now she doesn't have time for me," and things of that nature.

As an entrepreneur you'll spend more hours working

than on an average nine-to-five job, but somehow everything about you bothers them, because they can't accept that some things must change. In your mind you must say, "Yes, I'm evolving. I'm embarking upon a new life, and some sacrifices must be made." The majority of the sacrifices are money and time. It's nothing personal. Family time and friend time is all the same; even "me" time goes by the wayside. Just like I did when saving money so my investments in stocks could increase, I started doing my own hair and nails; any other luxury items (well, except shoes, of course) were forbidden. Still, I did my best to juggle all of the events that landed on my calendar in bridal showers, weddings and baby showers, birthday celebrations, and special engagements. The fact still remained that time management was crucial, especially in the first five to seven years of starting a business.

The people on your side must understand that things will be a little different but only temporarily. Your true friends will be there during the storms as well as on the days when the sun shines brightly. Just like the Bible speaks of a tree that bears no good fruit, it goes without saying that in order for the tree to flourish, some of the branches need to be pruned; the rotten fruit is plucked. This extracting or "pruning" process was good for me and empowered me to end several long-term relationships with catty women, who I found through my current endeavors, had always secretly disliked me. As I released them with ease, comfort and joy, they were soon replaced with genuine love from my true friends and family who remained by my side. Just like those insecure business owners who shut the door directly on my pointed-toe stilettos, friends and associates turned foes could slide out of my life as easily as one could slip off a pair of mules. Once a woman, whose name escapes me, came to the shoe salon and spoke on the fact that people, like fruit, can ferment and become rotten if we hold onto them past their season. I was maturing, and it felt so good when I began repairing any side effects left from broken relationships in all forms.

April 28, 2005, was my deadline. I purchased the property at 4518 S. Cottage Grove as a condominium store front with an unfinished basement (then it was just a crawl space) and had it completely rehabbed in four months. Yes, there were some lingering moments of fear, absolutely; but I did it anyway. Fear could not stop what was ordained by God. Disobedience and not following my heart could halt everything, but I learned a technique that will be with me until there isn't a single breath left to flow through my lungs—encourage myself.

It was only a few days before the salon was set to open, and you have to know that no one could have been happier than I. Every naysayer criticized the location, told me the economy was too bad to start a business and every other negative thing that one could imagine. The eye that I kept on purchasing the right shoes to place on brand new glass shelves was the same one I kept on the prize.

The doorbell rang and I ran to the door, excited that I would be greeting my first new client. My new standard greeting, "Hi, welcome to Sensual Steps Shoe Salon. Are you looking for anything in particular?" flowed from my lips.

The angry man looked at me, heated disgust filling his eyes, as he asked, "What is this place?"

Taken aback, I managed to reply, "We are a women's shoe boutique." This man, who I had never seen before that moment, had the nerve to say, "Girl, why would you build this place on a block where there are no other businesses? You are bound to fail."

My heart froze. My mind stood still. The only thing that I could say was, "God will ensure my success." I wish I could scream to the world how detrimental negative words can be to someone. Even if you don't understand someone's vision or mission, even if you believe they are nuts for following their dreams, don't pour salt on them. Negative words are like poison in the minds of others. The more appropriate thing to say is, "Keep praying, and let God lead you." Tell them that you will be praying with them as well. Some don't know God's plans for their own lives, let alone someone else's. There aren't too many things that make me angry, but this one particular thing is like having a sliver of glass slipping around inside my shoes.

After I delivered my heart-felt answer to this total stranger, I locked the door. I lowered my head, looked down at my feet, and cried. Every ounce of courage and bravado, every ounce of faith slipped from my mind, heart and soul. "God, what am I doing? I've invested everything that I have into this place, and it is built on an abandoned block! Oh God, why have you forsaken me?" I cried really hard for about five minutes. At the lowest points in life, something so strong inside, like a surge of electricity, will flow through the body and force you to move.

After my crying spell, I felt a bolt hit me and I ran to the big, beautiful mirror in my store. I took a good look at myself and said, "He doesn't know who I am." My chin lifted as I followed with, "He doesn't know that this is God's plan for my life." That man, that *stranger*, had me twisted. I had put things in place to keep me going strong after the actions and words of friends and family who doubted my mission. How could I let him sway me? Once again, I was reminded that self-esteem can be an ongoing battle. Situations may arise to test it, to bolster it and to make you reflect. Every positive affirmation that my mind could gather at that moment came out of my mouth, counteracting his negative words . . . his angry energy. I didn't even realize that I was speaking positive affirmations. People sometimes knowingly, and unknowingly, can speak death into something of yours that God is giving life. Remain prayerful; listen to God's conscious voice. Block out the negative voices and stand strong.

Moments later, I was back on my toes ready for the show down. It was WAR! He would not be the only one who felt this way. I would have to quickly wrap myself around the fact that everyone had an opinion that could be entirely different from mine, but it did not mean that I have to value or act upon their feelings. Sesvalah, the author of *Speak It into Existence*, says when negative people come to you that way, it's best to say a simple, "Thanks for sharing, but that's not what I believe." When people call on the phone ready to dump gossip or pour salt on your plans, get off the phone as quickly as possible. Just say, "Girl, I'm in the middle of something right now" or "I'll have to call you back." Sesvalah is so right! I will definitely respect people because they are entitled to their opinions, but I will not carry the weight of their negative words on my shoulders or in my soul. That gives others too much power over my life.

The day of my grand opening, I placed a beautiful pink treasure chest near the front door so anyone could donate new and gently worn shoes for less fortunate women in shelters. Seven wonderful girlfriends and two staff members all anxiously waited on our new clients. The opening included shoe cakes, martinis, fashion shows, a live band and most importantly, all the lovely footwear that would provide an exciting shoe shopping experience. Everything was intact. We made more money than I could count in a single day!

A week after my grand opening, Janine provided me with a book entitled *The Dynamic Laws of Prosperity*, by Catherine Ponder.

She said, "Nicky, if you want your business to prosper, make God your business partner. Find out how by reading this book." Unfortunately, I was in a state of overload and tossed the book to the side with many other uplifting books that I received as boring gifts all the time.

Little did I know that right at that moment, when I tossed the book on the shelf with the others, I tossed away a key piece of my future.

When you read, you grow…you must feed your mind just as you feed your body.

Chapter 5:Ponder over these questions

It's time for a change now. You must push through your fears and build your mind to achieve your goals. What do you need to do differently? What must you change in your life? Is it your attitude? The old cliché, "Your Attitude will equal your Altitude" is true. Change your attitude about people today. Stop judging others. Find your inadequacies and turn them into strengths. Your thoughts control your actions. Choose to think positive thoughts.

Write down your thoughts in your journal

Let nothing dim the light that shines from within.
- Maya Angelou

CHAPTER 6

PUMP UP YOUR ACTIONS TO INCREASE IN EVERY AREA
OF YOUR LIFE.

We must get busy living and not dying. The words
we speak help or hurt us. Negative words are like
murder, or should I say that you "redrum" yourself...
Yes, this is murder spelled backwards. Does it make
sense to be the killer of your own dreams? No, it is
senseless to eliminate yourself from the great life you
deserve to have. You may feel like you're living on
the ground level of life with your mind in the cold
basement filled with unwanted thoughts and fears
of failure. Even though you desire to move from the
basement to the penthouse, you don't know how or
when to start.

Who have you chosen as friends? Think about
this and be honest with yourself. Are you hanging
around individuals for the sake of popularity? You
know they are not living right and participate in
negative, destructive activities. Remove yourself

from these so-called friends and get around some champion-minded individuals. Stop feeling inferior of others' greatness and begin to learn what makes them great. Changing your friends from negative minded, growth stunting people to highly imaginative, positive and goal-oriented people can transform your life. I am not judging anyone; it is not my job or yours to do so. It is important to surround yourself with successful people regardless of your internal fears. You must push yourself through challenging situations, because your future is being determined right now with every decision. Make the right choices; choose to remove yourself from the basement and aim for the penthouse.

Imagine it and then begin to work towards the goal…
it's possible

Only a mere five years later, I was completely down on my luck again. My store was losing more money than I could count. People stopped shopping because of the "recession," at least that's what the nation called it. Let's do the math. According to the U.S. Census, there are 97 million women between the ages of 18 and 64, and for my purposes, they all (typically) have feet. People make purchases every single day. This means there are customers ready to buy products. I had to release a negative mindset and tap into the energy and resources to reach them. When people start believing that there is a recession, negative thinking becomes an escape. It's the easy route to say that *everything in the world is going bad right now, so it's okay that I'm in this situation.* That mindset accepts failure, and even becomes comfortable with it.

There is something much bigger than the existence of this world. It's the Being that created it. What is His master plan for your life? He designed our lives to be filled with prosperity including great health, happiness, wealth and peace. Most of these areas are priceless and cannot be attained with money. When they are not in sync, chaos exists. When living in a state of chaos, God's voice can't be clearly heard. You need that inner peace to enjoy the time you have on this earth. Naleighna, an author and publicist, constantly says that, "God did not put us here for the sole purpose of paying bills! Some people get so caught up in the day to day things that they forget there is a higher purpose for everyone's life. We are all lessons and blessings to each other."

Good health is another major point. Without good health, energy levels can decrease and lead to problems that impact other areas of life. The body is a holistic unit, and what affects one part influences others. Previously, I thought prosperity was just about finances. I was completely wrong. Having experienced health challenges myself, I learned from personal experience the importance of a healthy body. Though I had plenty of money at the time, I couldn't get out of bed, which meant I couldn't spend or enjoy it. This experience helped me define true prosperity—how to have a great balance in my life and to transform defeatist or negative thinking into victory.

With a new perspective on life, another area needed rescuing: my finances. Overdraft fees alone were almost like paying another monthly mortgage. The credit cards were back up to their limits, and I couldn't keep a dime in my pocket. Business was slow and my remaining real estate investments faltered as tenants couldn't pay their rent. I could not believe it. I thought I was the most financially stable person and would remain that way for the rest of my life. Credit companies that previously extended lines of credit to me were now taking things away. The banks that made thousands of dollars from my business and investments refused to give me a bail-out program. Financial wealth and physical health were both diminishing, and money slipped through my fingers like grains of sand.

My focus was now wondering what else could possibly go wrong. I started to doubt myself, something I had not done in years. Janine, ever the positive one, said, "Nicky, snap out of this! God entrusted you with so much in the past. You have been so faithful in giving to others—and even now you haven't stopped tithing. God will not fail you now." Truthfully, she was getting on my last damn nerve (and is highly irregular for me to use foul language because it is not lady like), I felt that with everything I had accomplished up to this point, God deserted me.

Janine sat in the passenger seat of my car and asked me to go home and pick up the entrepreneurial finance book for her, the one that was written by Professor Steven Rogers. I pulled over in front of my house, darted inside, and looked for it without success. My books were normally in one central place, so I couldn't understand why I couldn't find this one. I tore through the house looking everywhere. I knew that if I didn't find that book, she would get on my nerves until I did. Janine was an avid reader. Out of over one hundred books on my shelf, I finally saw the one titled, *The Dynamic Laws of Prosperity*. I said, "Hmmmm, this sounds interesting. A little familiar, but interesting… I'm going to give her this book and shut her up."

The most peculiar thing happened as I skipped to the door. As soon as my shoe hovered over the threshold, I heard a voice. God's voice never sounds to me the way it would if someone was talking right across from me, and I instantly recognized it.

The voice was so loud and clear to me: "Nicole, *you* are going to read this book." I said, "No, no, no—oh no! I need some dinero, some cashola, some money from you, God. I'm not about to read this thick book. I don't have time. I need some *money!*"

God said again, in that same loud voice in my head, "You *will* read this book." The second time scared me a little. Now you can't hear God's voice the way you can hear your best friend talking to you on the cell phone, but it is a voice that touches your soul repeatedly until it is heard. I walked to the car, with a little less skip in my step, because now I had to break the news to Janine that I couldn't find the book she really wanted. Next I had to explain that God was demanding that I keep and read the book I actually found for her. Out of hundreds of books I own, I don't know what made me grab that one. So I got in the car and told Janine what transpired and ended with my experience at the threshold.

Janine lightly snatched the book from my hand. She did not have her reading glasses with her, so she held the book very close to her face and peeled through the pages. "Now Nicky, I gave you this book *four years ago*! I can't believe you haven't read a single sentence. There isn't even a pen mark in this book! I told you that if you wanted your business to prosper, God had to be your business partner." All I could do was apologize and commit to reading the book. I began that very day. This was the day when my life changed for the better. I decided to complete one chapter each day. After one week of reading the book, I could feel my faith and strength being restored.

The story in the Bible that warms my heart is a miracle of the empty vessels. A woman whose husband died, did not have anything—not even food for her children— only a small vessel of oil. She was commanded by

the prophet Elisha to borrow empty vessels from her
neighbors and then pour the oil from the small vessel she
had. As she poured, the oil miraculously kept flowing
until every single pot was filled. She told Elijah what
happened, and he instructed her to go sell the oil. With
the money she received, the woman was to pay the man
her husband owed and use the rest to buy food for herself
and her family.

    This story matched my life in many ways. My vessel
was empty, and a single book of wisdom, along with the
encouragement of a good friend, helped to fill all the
empty vessels in my life: the vessels of faith, hope, love
and prosperity.

    I called Janine again, (I always scream...) and I
screamed, "Janine there is help for us. You were right. I
apologize for having been so doubtful."

    Janine said, "It's okay. It wasn't your time then, but
it is certainly your time now."

    I understand now, as I had not before, that the book
and its powerful information would not have had as
great an impact on me until this low point in my life.
When one is down and in despair—like Job in the Bible
experienced with the loss of his home, his belongings,
his children—there is no place to go but up. Sometimes
it takes a book, a word, or a person. For me it was a
person who introduced me to a book with life-changing
information (four years before I needed it), for God to
say, "Listen up, woman!"

    So I'm saying to you, the young, energetic person
reading this book, "Listen up!" Open your mind because
you will not believe the next set of events that transpired.

    Somehow I had to convince Janine to step completely
out of her comfort zone. We have a great deal in common
. . . Janine is a shoe fanatic as well! Even though I'm
mentioning her in the Pump chapter, Janine is a straight-

up stiletto woman. Now let me also tell you that she is one of the most humble, loving, compassionate, spiritual, trustworthy and peaceful women I have ever met. She is a walking book filled with so much knowledge, but *she did not like to speak publicly*.

Ironically, we both paid for a speech coaching class but didn't take the time to attend. We both knew that it was in Divine Order for us to do a lot more speaking engagements; I would put Janine on the spot quite often at community events. This practice should have served as a subtle warning for her. One day I called her knowing she wasn't going to like what I had to say.

"You must start conference calls next week! There are people out there hurting. They need to understand the power God gave them and need someone trustworthy like you to help them."

There was silence on the other end of the line, so I continued with, "As much as I love you, I can't just have your wisdom all to myself any longer."

When Janine spoke of spiritual things, she had a way of making people feel like they were the only ones who mattered in the world at that moment. She supported me through financial difficulties, marital issues and many other life situations. There are so many things I learned from these experiences: one of which is that spiritual and personal development is an ongoing process. It is not something accomplished in just one sweep of a year, two years, or even a decade. The same type of outward growth experienced as we go from a child to a teenager and later an adult is the same type of growth that occurs internally as we mature. Consequently, it goes without saying that every challenge, every milestone, every experience is all designed to help us reach the next level of spiritual development. We take the life's lessons with us to help get to the next level and gain wisdom along the way.

Let's just say that Janine, with a little resistance, agreed to the conference call idea. I called our backbone right away—my girlfriend, Tiffany. Janine is courageous, a risk-taker, positive and very vocal in personal settings. Tiffany, on the other hand, is more calm, humorous and feisty. What they have in common, however, is their spiritual foundation. Tiffany is a classic pump woman, but like Janine, won't go too far out of her element. Tiffany is like the outside of an Oreo cookie, and Janine is the center. I, on the other hand, am more of an Almond Windmill cookie. Either way, just like your favorite cookie, women can be sweet, different, a mouthful and unexpected. When people meet my two closest friends, they often say I am blessed for having such good people around me. Remember the old saying, *it takes one to know one*? My reply is that you must first **be** a good friend to **have** a good friend. My friends and I were beginning another journey that would lead to many wonderful opportunities. I grew more and more excited each day.

First, I contacted women and men who I knew were hurting financially, mentally or spiritually—it didn't matter which. I called every one I could and told them about our new conference calls and that they were free of charge. Janine ordered the books we would use on a wholesale basis and we began a spiritual movement that has helped change the lives of every person involved. In short, women and men that had been about to lose their homes were suddenly no longer in foreclosure. People who lost their jobs became employed. People who were mentally broken found stability and strength.

Collectively, we pulled together, prayed together and learned together. There's a big reason we took the time and do this without charging a dime. I read something recently that speaks to this point. Louise L. Hay, in her book, *Empowering Women*, states that if you focus on doing the thing you love, the money will follow.

Next, everyone built a vision board to map future goals. My board displayed the following items, and behind each request was a strong affirmation that I read every single day:

1) faith and favor restoration;

2) lifelong prosperity, no more temporary financial gain;

3) happiness, health and true love;

4) Sensual Steps, Inc.—to have an innumerable company of angels to work there and clients to shop;

5) to sell my home;

6) to be on a reality show on a major television network station that played into the homes of at least 10 million viewers.

Number six was kind of farfetched, but I now realize that there is no request that can be made to the Creator that is not without His ability to manifest.

Would you believe because of number one on my vision board, faith and favor restoration, that in the words of Naleighna Kai, "doors of opportunity were opening faster than I could walk through them."

Tiffany, Janine and I began a journey that is still changing our lives and the lives of others. We still conduct morning conference calls on a daily basis and invite people on a mission for change and praying, and then working until something happens.

With this in mind, I applied for a reality television show by submitting a video application. Would you believe that a network television station called me back! I even flew to Los Angeles for five days of taping. Then I made it to another stage in the application process so they came to the comfort of my home to film a private shoe soiree and later to visit my business. The taping was amazing. Every day I kept waking up wondering if I was dreaming or not. When this happened, God pinched me on the shoulder and say, "Yes, you are living this dream…it is real."

Not only was everything on my vision board coming to fruition, but the number of callers on our conference line grew immensely; even more men began to join us. I witnessed miracle after miracle simply because people dared to do something different. It's a simple notion that reading a book, praying, trusting, and believing in God's word, could enhance every aspect of life. Notice that the first focus was on the spiritual development, and then everything else followed. The focus wasn't on money or finding a way out of all the issues that almost knocked me off my feet. It was all about my connection to God and strengthening that connection through daily committed actions: prayer, affirmation, reading networking and sharing.

After making it to the final stages of being on a large network station, the only thing that came to mind was, "How could God do something so big for little old me?" I kept believing that these dreams were too big and belonged to someone else. I saw everyone else as a giant and viewed myself in miniscule terms. But let me tell you this, God makes no distinction between the two. It's the main reason David was able to slay Goliath—— he found favor with God and recognized God first and foremost. Size had nothing to do with it—faith and action, hand in hand, helped to slay the giant in David's life—and moved mountains in my own.

My journey felt a great deal like Moses in the wilderness leading the Hebrews from captivity to safety. Many of them saw the Promised Land in different ways. When the scouts went to check out the land and came back with their report, only two of them believed God's promise. The others feared the giants and expresses defeat and failure. Moses listened to both reports but acted on the one that would fulfill God's promise. Although he never made it to the Promised Land, his faithful follower, Joshua took the lead. At Jericho the walls came tumbling down, without him even lifting his sword and triumphantly led the Children of Israel into the Promised Land, their destiny.

We, too, have the ability to bring down the walls of Jericho in our lives—low self-motivation, lack of opportunity, procrastination, fear—all these things have contributed to the shaky foundation that frequently overpowers our very existence.

I'm sure that those Biblical warriors, the Children of Israel who walked around the stone-walled city seven times, did so in everything from bare feet to sandals. Now people of today can take the same walk of faith in Stacy Adams, Timberland, pumps, mules, stilettos or whatever keeps them jumping over hurdles and challenges.

Step on, young people. Step on!

Chapter 6: Ponder over these questions

Now is the time to start doing! Respecting your parents/ guardians and **following the rules** of your household is a requirement. You are still young waiting to blossom into a magnificent piece of artwork. However, you have stepping stones to cross in your life. You're not a child, but not yet an adult. If you step too far ahead before your time, you could possibly miss out on true prosperity. No, it is not very easy to change, but it is possible. Begin to respect your TEACHERS. Stop trying to be the class clown, who rarely gets anywhere in life. Stop trying to be the tough girl or tough guy. Put your strengths into other areas like improving your grades. No, it is not an option any longer to sleep around, do drugs, or put yourself right in the arena with others who don't honor you as a person. CHANGE your thoughts, and prosperity, on every level, will follow. So, you're saying it's not easy—nothing in life is, but you must do it anyway.

Live while you live. Not to go out and do your best is to sacrifice the gift.

- Steve Prefontaine.

CHAPTER 7

STILETTOS
Begin to Walk Tall…Take the High Road in Life

My life had taken another major turn. I made a decision to say, "NO MORE— no more mental abuse, no more settling for less, no more consistent unhappy days, and no more lack of peace." The power of saying "no more" provided the energy to change every single aspect of my life. I embraced each morning, expressed appreciation to God, even before brushing my teeth; and showed gratefulness for life and breath. Every day brought new expectations and opportunities; this was exciting.

When mistakes are made, you have two options: you can either bury yourself in shame or pain or feel defeated, or you can understand that, as the *Magic Story* says, failure only exists in the grave. Keep this one statement in mind: "Since I'm still living, there's still room for growth, for forgiveness (of myself and others) and building a new me." I am told that all of the cells in the body are rejuvenated every seven years, which means that on a cellular level, there's a new physical you. Now what would happen if there is just a single thought or series of thoughts that transform the mental, emotional and spiritual you? You don't have to wait several years to implement change. Why not start this very moment?

It's just like going out and purchasing a new pair of shoes and putting them on for the first time; it feels so good wearing them and having other people comment on how they look on your feet. It just feels good. A new way of thinking can provide you with that same feeling, one that complements your life and celebrates your journey. I could wake up every single day of my life, whether I ever bought another pair of shoes, or not and feel so good on the inside. You can, too!

After making God my business partner and speaking positive affirmations over my business, a multitude of good things began to flow. My almost poverty stricken life shifted and was filled with prosperity. Doors opened and connections began to manifest. Why? The only limitations that we have in life are the one's that we embed in our minds. We limit our opportunities by not believing in the infinite possibilities we have to enhance our lives. Students in my classes often say, "I can't stop cursing, yelling or screaming at others if they offend me, because they will think I'm weak." Well, I must tell you that you are weak-minded if you believe that rhyming curse words and being the loudest out of the group is going to help you maintain a certain level of being "cool" or maintaining popularity. Let me explain an important secret to you…while you are working so hard to be a class clown, others are laughing at you not with you, because you exude low self-esteem and lack good character.

Many other timid teenagers refuse to interact with their peers for the exact same reason; they fear not being accepted or respected. When people are loud, rude, and bossy that simply means they are acting as if they have no home training and are trying to impress people instead of focusing on being their very best.

Self-image is important. We all should walk like kings and queens and embrace all that has been placed on this magnificent earth. You must be who you were designed to be…if not, it's like living life as a beautifully wrapped gift that can never be opened. What good is a gift that only sits and looks pretty? What is in the inside when you open it? Untie the ribbon, take the lid off the box, and gain access to the wonderful gifts that are stored inside of you.

On a daily basis, we should ensure that our appearance (clothing, shoes, hair, nails and body odor) is in order. Get up and make yourself look good, because you will feel better after taking the time to enhance your outer appearance as you are working to build your inner appearance (thoughts, positive energy and new attitude). Cleaning our insides means removing emotional distress, negative thoughts and pessimistic people. These things suck our liveliness and drain our energy. You must increase your faith and take the word "CAN'T" out of your vocabulary. You can no longer be a beautifully wrapped gift under a tree that is never opened. You are too valuable to waste your gifts.

Accept that at times your heart will beat too fast. There will be an internal race going on within your mind – the negative chatter against the bold and bodacious positive person that exists within you. The race is fear against faith, and at times you will not know which one will hit the finish line first. No more compromising decisions in your life. WRONG is WRONG…RIGHT is RIGHT. Choose the right path, because the wrong one will surely lead to a dead end. No more justifying your actions and making excuses for inappropriate behavior or poor choices. These are no real reasons. You are not bringing up your grades, or you can't stand everyone in the world. Take your finger, point it in your own direction, and correct yourself. That is the only person you have control over. Your thoughts will manifest into something either positive or negative. This manifestation can be the beginning of something new and amazing or a tragic ending. Life is filled with what I call the "decision making process." Decisions can make or break you.

The enemy inside and around each of us does not want us to prosper or progress. Our opponent is a dream killer who wishes to lay dormant in our psyche anticipating our demise. If you are ready to change your life and create phenomenal relationships with your parents, friends, and others, then change your thoughts about how you see them. Negative thoughts can and will ruin us if we do not take control of them. Positive thoughts have the ability to change the very essence of our lives, in every way. Thoughts are powerful and precede our actions.

I want to share a story with you that I heard recently. There was a 21 year old woman who lost the use of her legs. It was a devastating experience, and without any preparation for her mental state to deal with such a tragedy, she would not walk again. Needless to say, her condition took a major toll on her state of mind and also her family, because they could not understand why this happened to their daughter. Can you even begin to imagine walking one day and the very next day being in a wheelchair? The doctors declared that she would never walk again, but her mother had a very small seed of faith. When the woman received the doctors' report, giving up felt like the only available option. This situation broke her life into parts which were difficult to repair. In thinking about this young lady's life, I realized that if you allow your energy to focus on what is broken instead of solutions on how to pull it back together, there is a strong possibility healing and restoration will not occur.

Back to the story...this young and beautiful lady said, "I refuse to quit I will walk." Her mother declared with her every day loudly and confidently, "You will walk, you will run, you will dance." EVERYDAY... throughout the day. The daughter declared regardless of the doctors' report, "I will walk, I will run, I will dance." Even during the darkest hours, they both declared that she would "WALK, RUN and DANCE." Less than a year later, one day she was overcome with incredible faith beyond her imagination, she woke up and just began walking. Yes!

Your words have extreme power. The statement, "What you speak about is what you bring about" is completely factual. That young woman was able to bring forth a miracle in her life by speaking it aloud, believing in herself and rejecting fears or failure. She chose to live a courageous, bold life filled with only a glimpse of hope to change her situation in the face of many uncertainties. She took a chance to think something different, to say something unique and finally to focus on her faith.

I don't expect you to change instantly, but day-by-day you can implement these small affirmations into your life and mix them with good thoughts to bring about a life filled with greater happiness. There is a divine plan for you here on earth, and you must ask that it be revealed to you step-by-step. You are the only limitation in your life—no one else. Accept this fact now, and recognize you can change your life starting right now. BE WHO YOU WERE DESIGNED TO BE.

Chapter 7:Ponder over these questions

Walk tall and blossom into the divine, purpose-filled life that is waiting on you. Write out your goals for this year, and work vigorously to obtain them. Be specific and don't feel as if you can't have big dreams and achieve them. The world belongs to you...now embrace it.

Write out the goals in your journal.

Yesterday is history, tomorrow is a mystery, today is the present, that's why it's a gift. You may be disappointed if you fail, but you are doomed if you don't try. You may be only one person in the world, but you may also be the world to one person. You must be the change you wish to see in the world.

- Mahatma Gandhi

Daily Quotes for Encouragement and Motivation

Nothing in life is for Free…so Work Hard.

Be Afraid, but do it ANYWAY.

When life throws you lemons, make lemonade. Don't cry.

If you make a mistake, don't continue to ponder over it. Forgive yourself and move forward.

You have the power to change anything if you simply believe.

One of the most powerful words in the world to me is, "Believe."

Speak a positive affirmation to yourself. Daily scream out loud if you must, but speak it into existence.

Life is filled with opportunities. Don't let a good one pass you by because of fear.

The moment you stop dreaming will feel like the day you stop breathing.

Failure is only determined once you make it in your grave.

Claim victory for yourself. "Let my unlimited blessings appear now."

Quitting is absolutely not an option.

There will be strife with others, but speak positive existence back into the situation, and it will fix itself.

Gossip is for immature women without business…if you are a gossiper get some business quickly.

Being negative gets you nowhere fast…slow things down, relax and be positive.

With God you truly can do all things. Trust Him and put your foot down on the matter.

Be proud of who you are, and never let others tear your spirits down.

You have options in your life. Make the right decision

How can you desire a man of your own while you are with someone else's? This is like water and oil . . . it doesn't mix.

As long as you have breath in your lungs to live another day, embrace your unlimited opportunities.

Forget about the mistakes of your past, forgive yourself and start from where you are.

Nicole Jones

Highly-inspired Nicole Jones is the founder of Sensual Steps, Inc., author of *Dare to Walk In My Shoes* Confessions of A Sole Queen and *Dare to Walk in the Shoes Designed for YOU Teenage Edition*. She is also the owner of NJ Management Company, a property rehabilitation, real estate management and development company. Nicole also hosts monthly seminars and events catered to the growth and development of women, a passion she has harbored for the past fifteen years. As chairman and founder of Sensual Steps, Nicole has unearthed one of her many great talents - seeking out beautiful, sensual and unique shoes that women can feel proud about wearing. Having discovered a demographic that was fashionable, yet underexposed, and underrepresented in the Bronzeville community, Nicole aimed to break the mold by offering this growing population of stylish women distinctive and inspirational fashion embedded with an unmistakable hint of sensuality.

Nicole has appeared on NBC, ABC, CLTV, WFLD, FOX, The Steve Harvey Show, Jet and Ebony Magazine, Footwear News publication and other media outlets. She is known nationally as the Shoe Lady. Women admire her consultation and ability to assist them with surfacing their shoe craze, while building their self-esteem from simple, affordable and uniquely designed shoes.

Nicole, who has been a Motivational Speaker for fifteen (15) years with the Chicago Public Schools, is a graduate of DePaul University with a Bachelor of Arts in Business Management, and has earned the Urban Public Policy Certificate of Graduate Studies at the University of Illinois. In 2008, she completed her Master of

Arts degree with honors in Applied Professional Studies at DePaul University with a focus on "Urban Studies." In addition, she has received many awards and accolades for community contributions from: Breast Cancer Awareness; Weight, Health and Nutrition Programs; Women Finding Internal Peace; Financial Freedom; Prosperity Focus; and many other special programs that have helped hundreds of women reach towards and obtain a better quality of life. Her awards include: 1999 Diversity Advocate Award Recipient; 2005 Phenomenal Woman Award; 2006 Chicago's Mayor Office Neighborhood Hero Award; 2006 NU Bronzeville Business Award; 2007 Chicago Defender 50 Women of Excellence Award; 2007 Successful Graduate of the Chicago Urban League Next One: Building Next Generation of Business Leader's program; and 2008 National Honor Society Inductee.

All the odds were against this young, African American female who grew up on the south side of Chicago with nothing more than integrity and the drive to succeed. Though surrounded by poverty and despair, she refused to settle for less than her potential. Armed with the belief that everyone has a preordained purpose, she stepped out on faith to become an "Ordinary Woman, Doing Extraordinary Things."

LaVergne, TN USA
19 December 2010
209392LV00006B/80/P